OBEYING THE TRUTH

OBEYING THE TRUTH

Discretion in the Spiritual Writings of
Saint Catherine of Siena

Grazia Mangano Ragazzi

OXFORD
UNIVERSITY PRESS

OXFORD
UNIVERSITY PRESS

Oxford University Press is a department of the University of Oxford.
It furthers the University's objective of excellence in research, scholarship,
and education by publishing worldwide.

Oxford   New York

Auckland   Cape Town   Dar es Salaam   Hong Kong   Karachi
Kuala Lumpur   Madrid   Melbourne   Mexico City   Nairobi
New Delhi   Shanghai   Taipei   Toronto

With offices in

Argentina   Austria   Brazil   Chile   Czech Republic   France   Greece
Guatemala   Hungary   Italy   Japan   Poland   Portugal   Singapore
South Korea   Switzerland   Thailand   Turkey   Ukraine   Vietnam

Oxford is a registered trademark of Oxford University Press
in the UK and certain other countries.

Published in the United States of America by
Oxford University Press
198 Madison Avenue, New York, NY 10016

Library of Congress Cataloging-in-Publication Data
Mangano Ragazzi, Grazia.
[In obbedienza alla verit?. English]
Obeying the truth : discretion in the spiritual writings of Saint Catherine of Siena /
Grazia Mangano Ragazzi.
pages cm
Includes bibliographical references and index.
ISBN 978-0-19-934451-2 (hardcover : alk. paper)—ISBN 978-0-19-934452-9
(ebook) 1. Catherine, of Siena, Saint, 1347-1380. 2. Discretion. I. Title.
BX4700.C4M3213 2013
248.4—dc23
2013024411

1 3 5 7 9 8 6 4 2
Printed in the United States of America
on acid-free paper

To the life and innocence of children,
born and unborn.

For at the moment the sound of your greeting
reached my ears,
the infant in my womb
leaped for joy.

(Lk.1:44)

CONTENTS

PART TWO
ANALYSIS
Textual Examination: The Meaning and Role of Discretion in Catherine's Writings

PART THREE
COMPARISON IN HISTORICAL PERSPECTIVE
The Origins of Catherine's Discretion: From the Tradition of *Discretio* and Prudence to the Synthesis of Thomas Aquinas and the Reflections by Some of Catherine's Contemporaries

PART FOUR
SYNTHESIS
Discretion between Mysticism and Morality

PREFACE

Writing on discretion and prudence today risks generating misunderstandings. Each of the two terms is polysemic, conveying hardly reconcilable ideas. Even a cursory checking online of the *Oxford English Dictionary* reveals that *discretion* is the ability to discern right from wrong but can also signify, in a different context, circumspection. Likewise, if *prudence* is the ability to recognize and follow the right course of action (thus being the virtue that directs all human acts), the prevailing use of the term today is that of reserved behavior or inaction, even when the truth is under attack. In other words, *discretion* and *prudence*, far from signifying an attitude of courageous witness to the truth, have largely become synonyms with *timidity*, if not outright connivance in sin. This latter sense is so prevalent in common parlance that one can predicate of the contemporary use of the terms *discretion* and *prudence* what Clive Staples Lewis has called "verbicide."[1] This murder (or attempted murder) of a word (or at least its original or nobler meaning) is, obviously, not a merely linguistic phenomenon. When it aims at eliminating the meaning that points to the distinction between good and evil, verbicide denotes a

---

1. C. S. Lewis, *Studies in Words* (2nd ed.), Cambridge, 1967, p. 7.

profound social malaise, as John Paul II stressed with respect to the attacks on the unborn: against the use of ambiguous terms resulting in glossing over the tragic and unjustifiable reality of abortion, it is necessary "to have the courage to look the truth in the eye and to call things by their proper name, without yielding to convenient compromises or to the temptation of self-deception."[2] If there is a mystic whose characteristic trait is looking the truth in the eye and calling things by their name, this is certainly Catherine of Siena. Her teaching on discretion/prudence is indissolubly linked to her search for the truth and the ensuing action from having found it. This aspect needs to be emphasized at the outset, lest the prevailing contemporary use of the terms *discretion* and *prudence* deceive those approaching Catherine's writings.

A second preliminary warning is needed to dissipate possible confusion. One of the best known scholars on Catherine, the late Giuliana Cavallini, once remarked that Catherine has much to say to the contemporary world because in her there are at one time the best tendencies of our age and the firm reaction against its worst degenerations: Catherine knew that lying is always at war with the truth and that "one cannot love what is good without hating what is evil."[3] In other words, being meaningful to the contemporary world does not consist in sweeping under the carpet its errors, but speaking the truth even (and especially) when this requires denouncing with courage the evil that our time falsely calls good. This is indeed the highest form of charity toward our neighbors. As Benedict XVI wrote in his third encyclical, "*[o]nly in truth does charity shine forth*" because, without truth, "charity degenerates into sentimentality. Love becomes

---

2. Encyclical letter *Evangelium Vitae* (March 25, 1995), in *L'Osservatore Romano* (English edn., April 5, 1995), para. 58. (The original Latin text is in *Acta Apostolicae Sedis* 87 (1995), pp. 401–522.) On Pope John Paul II's fight against the mystification of language, see W. Brennan, *John Paul II: Confronting the Language Empowering the Culture of Death*, Ave Maria, FL, 2008.

3. G. Cavallini, *Caterina da Siena—La verità dell'amore*, Roma, 1978 (reprint 2007), pp. 58–59.

an empty shell, to be filled in an arbitrary way. In a culture without truth, this is the fatal risk facing love."[4] In Catherine's writings, there is no trace of sentimentality precisely because she forcefully teaches that the truth is not to be sought through an indefinite sentiment of peace and love (the "empty shell" in Benedict XVI's incisive expression) but is known in the concrete exercise of the moral virtues enlightened by grace. Catherine's spirituality has its roots in the virtuous life and in obedience to the truth, which God has revealed to man and imprinted in his heart. The very reference to "obeying the truth," in the title of this study, in addition to capturing Catherine's teaching on discretion/prudence, underlies her scriptural inspiration, which animates all her spirituality.[5] In the same vein, the *predella* by the Sienese Duccio di Buoninsegna on the cover of this book expresses vividly Catherine's continuous call to conversion to Christ the Truth because, as Pope Francis so cogently preached in his very first homily quoting Léon Bloy, "he who does not pray the Lord prays the devil."[6]

Having cleared the deck of these possible misunderstandings, I need clarify only one point of style. There is perhaps no better time than this for publishing in English on Catherine's spirituality, as the translation of the whole body of her writings has now become available. In my quoted passages from Catherine's writings, I have of course used the most recent translations, indicating in square brackets those changes that I deem appropriate for greater consistency with the Italian originals. (Most important, for the reasons that will be given in this study, *discretion* remains in my view a better

4. Encyclical letter *Caritas in veritate* (June 29, 2009), in *L'Osservatore Romano* (English edn., July 8, 2009), para. 3. (The original Latin text is in *Acta Apostolicae Sedis* 101 (2009), pp. 641–709.)

5. "Obeying the truth" echoes this biblical passage: "Having purified your souls by your obedience to the truth for a sincere love of the brethren, love one another earnestly from the heart. You have been born anew, not of perishable seed but of imperishable, through the living and abiding word of God" (1 Peter 1:22–23).

6. Homily by the Holy Father Pope Francis, Sistine Chapel, March 14, 2013, available in Italian at www.vatican.va.

translation than *discernment* for the Italian *discrezione*.) At the same time, in the notes, I have also retained the reference to the Italian originals to facilitate the reader's approach to Catherine's own text, which remains the inescapable point of departure for serious study, irrespective of how good any translation may be.

Finally, as is invariably the case for writers, I have incurred a significant debt of gratitude toward teachers and friends, whose names are too many to be listed here. Cynthia Read, Executive Editor at Oxford University Press, ably assisted by Charlotte Steinhardt, Assistant Editor, and the copyeditors, led the process of publication of this book with admirable patience and efficiency. I also wish to thank John A. Di Camillo, B.E.L., a fine ethicist of whose outstanding command of English and Italian I have taken advantage. My husband, Dr. Maurizio Ragazzi, has provided me with the intellectual contribution and moral encouragement that only marital love can inspire. Above all, I am grateful to Christ for the incomparable gift of his Body and Blood, who daily nourishes me through his mystical body, the Church.

Dr. Grazia Mangano Ragazzi
Washington, DC, March 25, 2013,
birthday of Saint Catherine of Siena
(and solemnity of the Annunciation
if it were not falling during Holy Week)

ABBREVIATIONS

a(a).	article(s)
ed(s)., edn.	editor(s), edition
et al.	*et alii/et aliae*
etc.	*et cetera*
ch(s).	chapter(s)
col(s).	column(s)
ibid.	*ibidem*
i.e.	*id est*
No.	number
op. cit.	work cited
p(p).	page(s)
para(s).	paragraph(s)
q(q).	question(s)
tr.	translation
vol(s).	volume(s)

WRITINGS OF SAINT CATHERINE (ENGLISH)

Dialogue　　　Catherine of Siena, *The Dialogue* (S. Noffke, ed.),
New York, Ramsey, and Toronto, 1980.

Letters	S. Noffke (ed.), *The Letters of Catherine of Siena*, Tempe, AZ, 4 vols.: 2000, 2001, 2007, and 2008. (The first volume had initially been published in 1988.)
Prayers	S. Noffke (ed.), *The Prayers of Catherine of Siena* (2nd edn.), Lincoln, NE, 2001.

LIFE OF SAINT CATHERINE (ENGLISH)

Life	Raymond of Capua, *The Life of Catherine of Siena* (C. Kearns, ed.), Wilmington, DE, 1980.

WRITINGS OF SAINT CATHERINE (ITALIAN)

Dialogo	S. Caterina da Siena, *Il Dialogo* (2nd edn. G. Cavallini), Siena, 1995.
Lettere	Misciatelli, P. (ed.), *Le lettere di S. Caterina da Siena ridotte a miglior lezione e in ordine nuovo disposte con note di N. Tommaseo* (6 vols.), Siena 1913–1922 (reprinted in Florence, 1939–1940).
Orazioni	S. Caterina da Siena, *Le Orazioni* (G. Cavallini, ed.), Roma, 1978.

OBEYING THE TRUTH

General Introduction

1. WHY A STUDY ON CATHERINE OF SIENA?

One of the fundamental questions today, as the works of Cardinal Ratzinger and his later teaching as Pope Benedict XVI confirm,[1] is ascertaining what role Christianity still has in the Western world, and most notably Europe, as the central feature of its cultural and spiritual identity.

In the long history of holiness through the various regions of Europe over the past two millennia, a distinct component has been "feminine holiness," which led Pope John Paul II to elevate Saint Catherine to copatroness of Europe, together with Saint Bridget of Sweden and Saint Teresa Benedicta of the Cross, in the imminence of the Jubilee year 2000.[2] This title was yet another one in the stream of those that Roman pontiffs had conferred on Catherine, including the title of Doctor of the Church,[3] through which Catherine had joined the exclusive circle to

1. See, for example, J. Ratzinger, "The Spiritual Roots of Europe: Yesterday, Today and Tomorrow," in J. Ratzinger and M. Pera, *Without Roots: The West, Relativism, Christianity, Islam* (M. F. Moore, tr.), New York, 2006, pp. 51–80. See also Benedict XVI's speech to members of the European Popular Party on March 30, 2006: "Key religious contribution: Enlightening consciences," in *L'Osservatore Romano* (English edn., April 12, 2006), p. 4.

2. Apostolic letter *Spes aedificandi* (October 1, 1999), in *L'Osservatore Romano* (English edn., October 6, 1999), pp. 8–10.

3. An English translation of Pope Paul VI's apostolic letter *Mirabilis in Ecclesia Deus* (October 4, 1970), whereby Catherine was conferred the title of Doctor of the Church, can be found at www.drawnbylove.com. (The original in Latin is in *Acta Apostolicae Sedis* 63 (1971), pp. 674–82.) The satisfaction of the requisites of eminent doctrine, holiness of life, and recognition by popes and councils is set forth in the *Informatio super dubio* in *Urbis et orbis concessionis tituli Doctoris, et extensionis eiusdem tituli ad universam Ecclesiam, necnon Officii et Missae de communi doctorum virginum, in honorem S. Catherinae Senensis, virginis, Tertii Ordinis S. Dominici (Sacra Rituum Congregatione, Michaele Browne, relatore)*, Città del Vaticano, 1969, pp. v–xxii.

which only one other female saint, Saint Teresa of Avila, had been raised before her, just a few days earlier.[4]

These elements alone would suffice to select Catherine's spiritual works as a subject of study. But there is more to it than that. Though distinctively medieval in her life, thought, and spirituality,[5] Catherine is truly a "wonder of all times,"[6] which is the reason her influence is not only "historically incontrovertible"[7] but has also never been interrupted over the centuries and has actually increased. Catherine still speaks to the men and women of today by the way she actively worked in the political and ecclesiastical life of her times without sacrificing an intense contemplative life.

4. Apostolic letter *Multiformis Sapientia Dei* (September 27, 1970), in *Acta Apostolicae Sedis* 63 (1971), pp. 185–92. Until that date, the Doctors of the Church had been thirty, all of them men. (Today they count four women: in addition to Catherine and Teresa, there are also Saint Thérèse of Lisieux (elevated in 1997) and Saint Hildegard of Bingen (elevated in 2012).) In view of the elevation of a woman to Doctor of the Church, a problem was the relationship between doctorate and Magisterium (reserved to the successors of the Apostles). This difficulty was resolved by a unanimous pronouncement of the plenary assembly of the then Congregation of the Rites on December 20, 1967. (See, on this point, the "*Declaratio promotoris generalis fidei*," in *Urbis et orbis*, op. cit., pp. 1–9, at p. 2.) On the theological significance of Catherine's elevation to Doctor of the Church, see G. Berceville, "La proclamation de Sainte Catherine Docteur de l'Église: une approche de théologie historique," in D. Giunta (ed.), *Il servizio dottrinale di Caterina da Siena*, Firenze, 2012, pp. 15–51.

5. "If she was not the greatest woman of the middle ages, she was certainly the greatest woman saint and mystic": B. Hackett, *William Flete, O.S.A., and Catherine of Siena*, Villanova, PA, 1992, p. 79.

6. This expression was coined in the seventeenth century by the Flemish Jesuit Cornelius a Lapide. See *Commentaria in duodecim prophetas minores, auctore r.p. Cornelio Cornelii a Lapide, e Societate Iesu*, Antverpiae 1685, ch. 9, para. 17, p. 728: "virgo angelica, & virgo talis, ut facta sit portentum sæclorum omnium."

7. D. Abbrescia and I. Venchi, "Il movimento cateriniano (saggio storico—spirituale—bibliografico)," in *Urbis et orbis*, op. cit., pp. 277–313, at p. 277. This is confirmed by the many artistic renditions of Saint Catherine throughout the centuries, on which see G. Kaftal, *St. Catherine in Tuscan painting*, Oxford, 1949; Sr. M. Jeremiah, *The Secret of the Heart. A Theological Study of Catherine of Siena's Teaching on the Heart of Jesus*, Front Royal, VA, 1995, pp. 177–200.

2. WHY A STUDY ON DISCRETION?

A study on the writings of an illiterate saint who dictated to amanuenses may seem odd. Yet, Catherine lives in the Church not only through the memory of her admirable life but also through her writings, which reveal a spiritual reflection of remarkable depth.

This is why, alongside a significant body of mainly hagiographic studies on her life, there are also a considerable number of studies on Catherine's writings, which are themselves part of the rich Italian literature of the fourteenth century. Her magnificent Italian, which is at one time concise and incisive, has drawn the interest of literary scholars, leading in turn to an abundant tradition of stylistic analysis of Catherine's writings.[8]

This study investigates whether discretion, to which Catherine dedicates chapters 9 to 11 of her *Dialogue* and letter 213,[9] may be a helpful (or even decisive) tool for interpreting the whole edifice

---

8. See, for example, J. Tylus, *Reclaiming Catherine of Siena: Literacy, Literature and the Signs of Others*, Chicago, 2009; C. Forbes, "The Radical Rhetoric of Catherine of Siena," in *Rhetoric Review* 23 (2004), pp. 121–40. In Italian, the classic studies remain those by Giovanni Getto (1913–2002): *Letteratura Religiosa del Trecento*, Firenze, 1967, pp. 109–267; *Letteratura e critica nel tempo*, Milano, 1968, pp. 117–91; and a study he had published thirty years earlier: *Saggio letterario su S. Caterina da Siena*, Firenze, 1939.

9. The numbering of Catherine's letters adopted in this study is the one found in the classic N. Tommaseo, *Le lettere di S. Caterina da Siena ridotte a miglior lezione e in ordine nuovo disposte con proemio e note di Niccolò Tommaseo*, 4 vols., Firenze, 1860. This first edition was later printed as P. Misciatelli (ed.), *Le lettere di S. Caterina da Siena ridotte a miglior lezione e in ordine nuovo disposte con note di N. Tommaseo*, 6 vols., Siena, 1913–22. This latter edition (as reprinted by Casa Editrice Marzotto in Florence in 1939–40) is the one followed for the Italian original text of the letters. Despite the undoubtful merits of the more recent S. Caterina da Siena, *Le lettere* (5th edn. U. Meattini), Milano, 1993, the reference text for scientific purposes has remained the one by Tommaseo (as edited by Misciatelli). One could certainly be critical of Tommaseo's edition, but to this day it is the only complete collection, thus remaining the standard one by default, given the "inadequacy of all the other ones" (F. Santi, "La scrittura nella scrittura di Caterina da Siena," in L. Leonardi and P. Trifone (eds.), *Dire l'ineffabile: Caterina da Siena e il linguaggio della mistica. Atti del Convegno (Siena, 13–14 novembre 2003)*, Firenze, 2006, pp. 41–69, at p. 48, note 6).

of Catherine's spirituality. To avoid any possible misunderstanding, throughout this study (but, obviously, not necessarily in quotations from other writers), the Italian term *discrezione* will be rendered with the English term "discretion," instead of "discernment" (which is how the term is often rendered in English). The reason for this choice is that, as will become clear from this study, the term *discernment* reflects only partially the fullness and complexity of discretion.

According to Giuliana Cavallini,[10] there is perhaps no "virtue which is as characteristic of Catherine as discretion.... [I]t is a characteristic feature of Catherine because of the prominence she attributes to it and the great extent to which she practiced it."[11] In spite of all this, the study of the concept of discretion in Catherine's spirituality remains almost virgin territory,[12] as is attested also by the fact that, among the many studies on Catherine's writings,[13] only a few specifically deal with discretion.[14]

---

10. Giuliana Cavallini (1908–2004), former director of what is now the International Center for the Study of Saint Catherine in Rome, played a fundamental role in spreading the knowledge of Catherine's spirituality and in promoting the restoration of the room (now a chapel) in Santa Chiara Square, Rome, where Catherine died.

11. G. Cavallini, "La voce di S. Caterina da Siena," in *L'Arbore della Carità* (1963), pp. 19–23, at p. 19.

12. This is the expression that Giuliana Cavallini used in a letter dated February 19, 1993, to the author of this study.

13. The bibliography on Catherine's writings and spirituality is so vast that "it frightens anyone embarking on a serious study" on Catherine (M. Zaggia, "Varia fortuna editoriale delle lettere di Caterina da Siena," in L. Leonardi and P. Trifone (eds.), *Dire l'ineffabile*, op. cit., pp. 127–87, at p. 127). Among the introductory studies available in English, see M. A. Fatula, *Catherine of Siena's Way* (revised edn.), Collegeville, MN, 1990; M. O'Driscoll, *Catherine of Siena—Passion for the Truth, Compassion for Humanity*, New Rochelle, NY, 1993; S. Noffke, *Catherine of Siena—Vision through a Distant Eye*, Collegeville, MN, 1996; G. Cavallini, *Catherine of Siena*, London and New York, 1998 and 2005; T. McDermott, *Catherine of Siena. Spiritual Development in Her Life and Teaching*, New York and Mahwah, NJ, 2008; G. D'Urso, *Catherine of Siena. Doctor of the Church (Notes on Her Life and Teaching)* (T. McDermott, tr.), Chicago, 2013.

14. In chronological order, these are the main studies specifically on the notion of discretion: T. Deman, "Commentaire théologique de la lettre 213 (éd. Tommaseo) sur la discrétion" (print-out from *Studi Cateriniani* 11 (1935)); A. Lemonnyer, "Il discernimento nell'insegnamento di S. Caterina," in *S. Caterina da Siena* 6 (1955, No. 6), pp. 8–15; F. Dingjan, "La pratique de la discrétion d'après les Lettres de Sainte

Hence the need for a monograph on this crucial concept to understand Catherine's spirituality.

3. STUDY PLAN AND METHODOLOGY

It is first of all necessary to ascertain whether one can talk of a truly Catherinian discretion, in other words, whether the concept of discretion can really be attributed to Catherine's own thinking as opposed to that of her amanuenses. The question arises from the fact that, despite the rather conspicuous literary production associated with her name, there are no autograph works, and the vast majority of Catherine's writings are found in manuscript collections attributed to her disciples. The first part of this study therefore examines the role that the amanuenses played in the composition of Catherine's writings[15] and whether it is possible to consider such writings as authentically reflecting her thought.

The second part then proceeds to a fairly detailed analysis of Catherine's works to determine the meaning and importance of discretion in her spirituality. After getting some preliminary responses from the analysis of selected passages from Catherine's *Dialogue*, the focus then shifts to her *Letters* and *Prayers*. The specific aim of this

Catherine de Sienne," in *Revue d'Ascétique et de Mystique* 47 (1971), pp. 3–24; S. M. Schneiders, "Spiritual Discernment in *The Dialogue* of Saint Catherine of Siena," in *Horizons* 9 (1982, No. 1), pp. 47–59; D. L. Villegas, *A comparison of Catherine of Siena's and Ignatius of Loyola's teaching on discernment* (Dissertation submitted in partial fulfillment of the requirements for the degree of Doctor of Philosophy in the department of theology at Fordham University, New York, 1986); D. L. Villegas, "Discernment in Catherine of Siena," in *Theological Studies* 58 (1997), pp. 19–38; G. Mangano Ragazzi, "La 'discrezione' nel *Dialogo* di Santa Caterina da Siena," in *Sacra doctrina* 54 (2009, No. 2), pp. 13–41; G. Mangano Ragazzi, *In obbedienza alla verità. La discrezione/prudenza come perno della spiritualità di Santa Caterina da Siena*, Siena, 2010. See also R. Spiazzi, "Il magistero politico di S. Caterina da Siena. Politica e coscienza," in *L'Osservatore Romano* (December 13, 1970), p. 6 (where the author identifies discretion as a key concept of Catherine's teaching).

15. For example, the eight originals of Catherine's letters were written by seven different hands, as an accurate examination of the writing reveals.

textual analysis is to clarify whether discretion truly holds a central place in Catherine's thought, which are its meaning and essential elements, and how it relates to the concept of prudence.

In the third part, the thorny issue to be addressed is that of the sources of Catherine's discretion. Though she was basically illiterate, Catherine was surrounded by "that intelligent and learned atmosphere that must have flowed through the heart of Catherine's circle."[16] The members of this learned circle included not only Dominican friars such as Raymond of Capua, Tommaso Caffarini, and Bartolomeo Dominici but also representatives of different spiritual traditions,[17] such as the Franciscan Gabriele da Volterra and Fra Lazzarino da Pisa, the Augustinian William Flete, and the Vallumbrosan Giovanni delle Celle. The clearest influence was certainly that of the Dominican spirituality: her spiritual director, Raymond of Capua, was a Dominican, as were the majority of those belonging to Catherine's circle. But Franciscan mysticism (which was prevalent in religious life during the thirteenth and fourteenth centuries) also seems to have exerted considerable influence on her writings, and perhaps even Benedictine

16. G. Getto, *Letteratura Religiosa*, op. cit., pp. 138–39.

17. This reference to different spiritual traditions raises the question of what sets apart one tradition from the others. In the footsteps of Thomas Aquinas, the Dominican friar P. Lippini wrote that it is their different aim that sets them apart. As to those traditions sharing the same aim, they will be distinguished from one another by their means. (*La spiritualità domenicana*, Bologna, 1987, pp. 42–44). On the Dominican character of Catherine's spirituality, Lippini adds that, even though Catherine may occasionally have borrowed from non-Dominican sources, the fact remains that it was from the Dominican order "that she learnt to love knowledge and that she got accustomed, as a woman, to reach God, not through the shaky way of sentiment, but through the sure way of doctrine" (ibid., p. 216). P. Murray calls Catherine's *Dialogue* "a Dominican text" (*The New Wine of Dominican Spirituality. A Drink Called Happiness*, London, 2006, p. 9, note 11). In the same vein, J. Pereira and R. Fastiggi have remarked that, in many ways, "Catherine provides Dominican spirituality with its most prominent and seductive expression" (*The Mystical Theology of the Catholic Reformation. An Overview of Baroque Spirituality*, Lanham, MD, 2006, p. 124). On Dominican spirituality, see also R. Garrigou-Lagrange, "Character and Principles of Dominican Spirituality," in A. M. Townsend (tr.), *Dominican Spirituality*, Milwakee, WI, 1934, pp. 57–82.

spirituality through the Vallumbrosan Giovanni delle Celle, as well as the spirituality of the Victorines through the Augustinian William Flete. The composite picture of Catherine's sources is certainly not limited to this learned circle. The wider background is the Christian tradition of *discretio spirituum* (discernment of the spirits) and *discretio* (discretion), tracing its origins to Scriptures (particularly the Pauline letters), later developed mainly by Cassian, Saint Benedict, and Saint Gregory the Great, and continued through to Saint Bernard and Richard of Saint Victor. Saint Thomas Aquinas, joining that tradition to Aristotle's teaching on prudence, would then achieve a magnificent synthesis of discretion and prudence.[18] In this third part, Catherine's discretion is compared with this tradition, with a view to assessing whether Catherine's concept of discretion encompasses both discernment and discretion proper, that is the moral virtue that, particularly from Cassian onward, would become the mother of virtues (*mater virtutum*). In comparing Catherine's concept of discretion with Aquinas's virtue of prudence, it is also interesting to note that, while since the thirteenth century the term *discretio* had come to be replaced by the term *prudence*, Catherine continued using the term *discretio*.

Catherine's way of being a theologian exemplifies the principle that any person authentically striving to live a Christian life, if gifted with great faith and intellectual prowess, can do theology in a creative manner without necessarily engaging in abstract and highly specialized speculation reserved for academics alone.[19] In this sense, the International Theological Commission's conclusion, in 1975, on how theology is done suits Catherine perfectly, in that the task of the theologian "derives its own force from the life of the Holy Spirit in the Church, which is communicated by the sacraments, the preaching of the Word of God, and the communion of love."[20] Catherine was a mystic theologian. Those

18. F. Dingjan, *Discretio. Les origines patristiques et monastiques de la doctrine sur la prudence chez saint Thomas d'Aquin*, Assen, 1967, pp. 2–3.

19. See M. O'Driscoll, "Catherine the Theologian," in *Spirituality Today* 40 (1988), pp. 4–17.

20. "Theses on the Relationship between the Ecclesiastical Magisterium and Theology," in M. Sharkey (ed.), *International Theological Commission. Texts and Documents 1969–1985*, San Francisco, 1989, pp. 133–48, at p. 138 (Thesis 7). The

studying Catherine's writings have always acknowledged this mystical aspect of her doctrine, just as hagiographers have attested her ecstasies (starting with Raymond of Capua's description of Catherine's state of ecstasy while composing the *Dialogue*), which are one of the defining moments of any mystical experience. It is therefore not surprising that Paul VI should emphasize the mystical charism of Saint Catherine in proclaiming her a Doctor of the Church. Accordingly, should this study reveal the importance of discretion as one of the key concepts in Catherine's thought, the final step in the fourth part will be to examine Catherine's discretion within the context of the relationship between mysticism and morality.

To determine the significance of discretion in Catherine's thought, one may be tempted to superimpose modern sensibilities on her writings, so as to translate her teaching into forms that are more consonant with contemporary theology. This temptation must be avoided. The difficulty in approaching Catherine's text, however, is that it is not structured in any systematic way.[21] Perhaps echoing the Latin maxim that no interpretation is needed for a clear text, Lonergan has remarked that "the more a text is systematic in conception and execution, the less does it stand in need of any exegesis."[22] Conversely, from this observation, one may infer that a nonsystematic text requires significant interpretative effort. How, then, should one approach Catherine's writings? A promising approach is to proceed, first of all, with an attentive analysis of Catherine's images and expressions and then clarify their meaning through a comparative approach that allows the identification of some at least (with no

International Theological Commission was instituted by Pope Paul VI in 1969 to assist the Congregation for the Doctrine of the Faith in its consideration of the doctrinal questions of greater weight.

21. D. Monteleone has remarked that Catherine, though solid in her doctrine, is not a "systematic" thinker: "Her rich doctrinal teaching is spread out in all her writings, and therefore calls for patient and meticulous investigation, if one wants to know and study it by thematic areas" ("Io, Caterina, confesso," in *Rivista di ascetica e mistica* 72 (2003), pp. 687–712, at p. 692).

22. B. Lonergan, *Method in Theology*, New York, 1972, p. 153.

presumption of listing them comprehensively) of the likely sources of the notion under investigation.

4. SALIENT EVENTS IN CATHERINE'S LIFE

On Catherine's life, there is an abundance of writings among which to choose, from hagiographical[23] and historical[24] biographies to shorter entries.[25] For the purposes of this study, it is sufficient to paint, with a wide brush, the key moments in the life of Catherine as they are

23. The principal work on Catherine's life, with hagiographical connotations, is Raymond of Capua's *Legenda maior*, reproduced in *Acta Sanctorum* (aprilis, t. III, pp. 862–967), and cited in this study in the English translation listed in the Abbreviations. There is also a *Legenda minor* by Tommaso di Antonio da Siena (Caffarini), of which there is an Italian translation by B. Ancilli, *S. Caterina da Siena— Vita scritta da fra' Tommaso da Siena detto "Il Caffarini,"* Siena, 1998. To the name of Caffarini is also linked the *Libellus de Supplemento. Legende prolixe Virginis Beate Catherine de Senis* (I. Cavallini and I. Foralosso, eds.), Roma, 1974, of which there is an Italian translation by A. Belloni and T. S. Centi, *Supplemento alla vita di S. Caterina da Siena*, Firenze, 2010. Finally, of fundamental importance is M.-H. Laurent (ed.), "Il Processo Castellano, con appendice di Documenti sul Culto e la Canonizzazione di S. Caterina da Siena," in R. Orestano et al. (eds.), *Fontes vitae S. Catherinæ senensis historici quos edidit Commissio editionibus Cathedrae Catharinae praefacta*, vol. 9, Milano, 1942, of which there is an Italian translation by T. S. Centi and A. Belloni, *Il Processo Castellano. Santa Caterina da Siena nelle testimonianze al Processo di canonizzazione di Venezia*, Firenze, 2009.

24. The better known biographies of the saint, available in English, are A. T. Drane, *The History of St. Catherine of Siena and Her Companions*, London, 1880 (4th edn. 1915); E. G. Gardner, *St. Catherine of Siena. A Study in the Religion, Literature, and History of the Fourteenth Century in Italy*, London and New York, 1907; A. Curtayne, *Saint Catherine of Siena*, London, 1934; S. Undset, *Catherine of Siena* (K. Austin-Lund, tr.), New York, 1954 (reprint, San Francisco, 2009); C. M. Meade, *My Nature is Fire: Saint Catherine of Siena*, New York, 1991.

25. Among these entries in English, see K. Foster, "Catherine of Siena, Saint," in *New Catholic Encyclopedia* 3 (1981), pp. 272–74; M. Jeremiah, "Catherine of Siena, St. (1347–1380)," in M. L. Coulter et al. (eds.), *Encyclopedia of Catholic Social Thought, Social Science, and Social Policy* 1 (2007), pp. 137–38; S. Noffke, "Catherine of Siena," in A. Minnis and R. Voaden (eds.), *Medieval Holy Women in the Christian Tradition c. 1100– c. 1500*, Turnhout, 2010, pp. 601–22.

summarized in a concise biography prepared by Dupré Theseider,[26] a well-known historian and expert on Catherine's writings.

(i) From Birth (1347) to the Departure from Her Domestic Cell (1367)

Catherine lived her thirty-three years in the second part of the fourteenth century, a time of "bloody and chaotic mess."[27] She was born in the Fonte Branda district of Siena to a dyer, Iacopo Benincasa, and to Lapa di Puccio Piagenti. The documents of the time do not identify her birthdate. According to tradition, and in the wake of the converging testimonies of Raymond of Capua, Caffarini, and the Anonymous Florentine, the year of her birth was 1347. The date usually given is March 25, the Feast of the Annunciation in the Catholic liturgical calendar and the New Year in the Sienese calendar, which that year coincided with Palm Sunday.[28]

Tradition also confirms that Catherine was quickly drawn to a mystic and contemplative life. At the age of six, while returning home, she had her first vision. In it, she saw Christ as pontiff in the act of blessing while on a throne surrounded by saints. This vision

26. E. Dupré Theseider, "Caterina da Siena, santa," in *Dizionario biografico degli italiani* 22 (1979), pp. 361–79. (The part on the life goes from p. 361 to p. 371, followed by an examination of Catherine's theology up to p. 378, and an ample bibliography.) Eugenio Dupré Theseider (1898–1975), an erudite historian who belonged to a Protestant family and was active in the Waldensian community in Rome, was charged with the task of preparing the critical edition of Catherine's letters. The first volume of this work was regarded as a model critical edition. On Dupré Theseider's contributions to the studies on Catherine, see E. Petrucci, A. Volpato, and S. Boesch Gajano, "Il contributo di Eugenio Dupré Theseider agli studi cateriniani," in D. Maffei and P. Nardi (eds.), *Atti del simposio internazionale cateriniano-bernardiniano. Siena, 17–20 aprile 1980*, Siena, 1982, pp. 255–70.

27. These are the words used by Simoni and cited in E. Dupré Theseider, *Problemi del Papato avignonese*, Bologna, 1961, pp. 100 and 102.

28. On Catherine's birthdate and the critical evaluation of certain arguments put forward by Fawtier, see E. Jordan, "La date de naissance de Sainte Catherine de Sienne," in *Analecta Bollandiana* 40 (1922), pp. 365–411.

made such an impression on her that she devoted herself to ascetic practices and took a vow of virginity.

In her early adolescence, apparently because of the influence of her sister Bonaventura, she had a slight vanity crisis that led her to dye her hair. But this "crisis" did not last long. In fact, the premature death of her sister led her to change her life and put on the habit of the Sisters of Penance of Blessed Dominic, who were referred to as the *mantellate* (cloaked) sisters on account of their black cloaks draped over a white tunic.[29] They were mainly devout widows, and Catherine became their first virgin member around 1364.[30]

Despite certain obstacles set before her in the family, Catherine persevered in her new life. She obtained a sort of domestic cell in her father's house, where she spent about three years in an ascetic and meditative life. Her confessors and spiritual directors were Dominicans: Angelo degli Adimari, Tommaso della Fonte, and Bartolomeo Dominici. Catherine went through mystical experiences during these years of meditation (such as her mystical marriage of faith) and improved her religious learning through daily contacts with her Dominican confessors and religious of other orders, including Franciscans and Augustinians.

It was also during these years that she read the lives of the Fathers (probably in the version by Domenico Cavalca), which served her as models of perfection. For example, the story of Saint Euphrosyne particularly struck her, and it is no coincidence that one of her disciples, Neri di Landoccio de' Pagliaresi, later composed the *Istoria di sancta Eufrosina* (Life of Saint Euphrosyne) in verse.

---

29. Catherine is occasionally described as a "Dominican tertiary." This expression, though, is inaccurate, as is clearly explained in A. Duval, "Sainte Catherine de Sienne 'dominicaine,'" in *La Vie Spirituelle* 134 (1980), pp. 827–51, at pp. 828–38.

30. R. Rusconi has written that, for a long time, Catherine remained "one of the many 'penitent women,' who in the Italian cities of the XIV century had entrusted themselves to the direction of the friars of the mendicant orders" ("L'Italia senza papa. L'età avignonese e il grande scisma d'Occidente," in A. Vauchez (ed.), *Storia dell'Italia religiosa. I. L'antichità e il Medioevo*, Bari, 1993, pp. 427–54, at p. 441).

(ii) From 1367 to the Beginning of Her Itinerant Apostolate (1374)

Catherine's vocation, however, was not as an anchorite: she was drawn to the lives of others and works of charity. The period of meditation just described was, in fact, followed by a period of intensive assistance to the sick and aid for the poor, in both material and spiritual terms. These were the years in which she had various mystical experiences: her heart becoming one heart with Christ's, her drinking from the wound in Christ's side, a rain of blood and fire purifying her, and Christ putting a nail through her right hand.

These were also the years in which a "Catherinian family" began to form spontaneously: a selected group of a few dozen devout people of respectable learning tied to Catherine like a mother. The group, which lacked any formal structure, included men and women, lay and religious, and people from both Siena and other parts of Tuscany.

Finally, it was during these years that Catherine began dictating her letters and becoming involved in political matters. Scholars do not discard the possibility that Catherine may have communicated with Urban V, who died in December 1370. It is clear, however, that she immediately entered into contact with his successor, Gregory XI, thanks to important ecclesiastical connections. By the beginning of the 1370s, Catherine was known in Siena and beyond as a woman who led a holy life in touch with the political situation of the time.

(iii) From 1374 to Her Experience at Tentennano Castle (1377)

The year 1374 was crucial for Catherine. It was when she began communicating directly with Pope Gregory XI. Some say that she was called before the General Chapter of the Dominican order in Florence in the spring of that same year to account for her actions;

however, others say this is simply due to erroneous interpretation of the Anonymous Florentine's writings.[31] Whatever the case, both her close relationship with Raymond of Capua as her spiritual director and the beginning of her itinerant apostolate date back to this same year.

Returning to Siena, she devoted herself to caring for those afflicted with the plague. In the autumn, she went to Montepulciano to venerate the body of Saint Agnes Segni. She traveled to Pisa early in 1375 in response to an invitation by the Captain-General and Defender of the Commune, Piero Gambacorti, who had written to her on behalf of several "holy women," and took up residence at the house of a noble, Gherardo de' Buonconti, next to the little Church of Saint Christina. On April 1, in the presence of Raymond of Capua and Bartolomeo Dominici, she received the stigmata of the Passion of Christ in this very church, asking and having it granted that they remain invisible.[32]

This same period included a mystical experience in connection with the execution of Nicolò di Toldo and her first letter to Gregory XI on the need to reform the Church, a recurrent theme in Catherine's spirituality. Catherine arrived in Avignon on June 18, 1376, presumably to speak with Gregory XI about several issues she had at heart, from her defense of the crusade to bringing peace to Italy, Church reform, and the return of the papal curia to Rome. It seems undeniable that Catherine's intervention had at least some persuasive effect on the pope, but historians disagree about various aspects of

---

31. See T. Centi, "Un processo inventato di sana pianta," in *Rassegna di Ascetica e Mistica* 4 (1970), pp. 325–42. The editors of the Italian edition of the Castellano Process (among whom is Tito Sante Centi, OP, brother of Timoteo Centi, OP) credit Timoteo Centi with having gotten rid of "that odd event, wiping it away once and for all from the biography of Saint Catherine of Siena" (T. S. Centi and A. Belloni (eds.), *Il Processo Castellano*, op. cit., p. 8).

32. See R. Garrigou-Lagrange, "La stimmatizzazione di Santa Caterina da Siena," in *Vita Cristiana* 9 (1937), pp. 37–54. Catherine's stigmata were at the origin of a lively dispute between the Dominicans and the Franciscans, into which the Franciscan Pope Sixtus IV intervened (A. Vauchez, *La sainteté en occident aux derniers siècles du Moyen Age d'après les procès de canonisation et les documents hagiographiques* (revised edn.), Rome, 1988, p. 487, note 21).

the reasons and results of her stay in Avignon. One way or another, Gregory XI left Avignon on September 13 and arrived in Rome on January 17, 1377.

In the meantime, Catherine had stepped back and devoted herself to working within the confines of Siena. In fact, she asked for and received permission from the General Council of the Commune to accept the ruins of a small fort (Belcaro) as a gift from a rich citizen and, with the permission already granted by the pope, to build a convent from it, which was dedicated to Saint Mary of the Angels.

At the end of the summer, Catherine traveled to Val d'Orcia on a mission to bring peace to two rival branches of the Salimbeni family. During her stay in Val d'Orcia, at the imposing Tentennano castle, Catherine lived an extraordinary experience of truth. She wrote about it to Raymond of Capua in letter 272.

(iv) From 1377 to Her Death in 1380

After the death of Gregory XI on March 27, 1378, Catherine rejoiced in the election of his successor, Bartolomeo Prignano, who would take the name Urban VI. She knew him from her time in Avignon and admired his moral rectitude.

Having run the risk of dying during the Revolt of the Ciompi in Florence, Catherine found herself in Siena for the last time in August 1378. It was there, according to Dupré Theseider, that she prepared the materials she had been collecting for the composition of the *Dialogue*, which first emerged as a literary work at this time.

On September 20, 1378, Clement VII was elected antipope in the town of Fondi by a group of dissident cardinals. This began the painful Western schism that would only be resolved in 1417.[33] Catherine immediately gave her full support to Urban VI, proclaiming his legitimacy without hesitation. In fact, she became the promoter of an

---

33. See J. Rollo-Koster and T. M. Izbicki (eds.), *A Companion to the Great Western Schism (1378–1417)*, Leiden and Boston, 2009.

initiative that met with the pontiff's favor: the convocation in Rome of important and holy members of the various religious orders on January 9, 1379. This idea, which the Italian writer Arrigo Levasti has called a "Council of ascetics and mystics,"[34] was not new for Catherine, since she had already proposed it during the pontificate of Gregory XI. Despite the initiative's failure, Catherine did not lose heart and continued her battle in defense of the Church and of the legitimate pope until her death.

From February to March 1380, Catherine went daily to Saint Peter's Basilica, spending the entire day in prayer for the Church and receiving the "mystical boat" on her shoulders as the seal of her ecclesial mission.[35] She died in Rome around noon on April 29, 1380, with Christ's dying words on her lips: "Father, into your hands I commend my spirit and soul."

(v) Tributes to Catherine after Her Death

The conclusion of her earthly life obviously did not draw the curtain on Catherine. From 1411 to 1416, an investigation into Catherine's virtues and her already ongoing veneration was conducted by the Diocese of Castello in Venice (from which the expression *Processo Castellano*, or "Castellano Process," derives).[36]

---

34. A. Levasti, *My Servant, Catherine* (D. M. White tr.), Westminster, MD, 1954, p. 328.

35. Regarding this period in Catherine's life, there is, of course, the question of what the situation in Rome was back then and, in particular, which role mendicant orders played in its ecclesiastical life. A. Vauchez has remarked that, given the opposition of the secular priests, mendicant orders did not play any signficant role before the fourteenth century, and the "lay confraternities came to light only after 1350, namely a century later than in the other Italian cities" (*Storia di Roma dall'antichità a oggi. Roma medievale*, Bari, 2001, p. xxix).

36. At the Castellano Process, twenty-three depositions were collected (in addition to two complementary notes and one letter) regarding Catherine's virtues and the cult that the people were already tributing to her. The Castellano Process, though, was not a canonization process. For Catherine, the latter took place only in 1461, thanks to Pope Pius II who entrusted three cardinals (Bessarion, Alain de Cœtivy, and Prospero

The canonization trial itself began in 1461 under Pius II, and she was proclaimed a saint in the Vatican Basilica on June 29 of that same year, following his letter, *Misericordias Domini*.[37] On April 13, 1866, Pius IX raised Catherine to saint patroness of Rome, alongside the Princes of the Apostles, through his *Quamvis Urbs Roma*. In his apostolic letter *Licet commissa* dated June 18, 1939, Pius XII then elevated Catherine to the status of primary patroness of Italy, alongside Francis of Assisi.[38] Paul VI recognized her as a Doctor of the Church on October 4, 1970, with his apostolic letter *Mirabilis in Ecclesia Deus*, and, on October 1, 1999, during the Second Special Assembly for Europe of the Synod of Bishops, John Paul II raised her—together with Bridget of Sweden and Teresa Benedicta of the Cross—to copatroness of Europe with his apostolic letter *Spes aedificandi*,[39] joining copatrons Benedict, Cyril, and Methodius.

Mentioning some of Catherine's more significant honorary titles throws light on how Catherine has continually been recognized as a model of holiness for all times, entire nations and peoples having been entrusted to her spiritual guidance and intercession.

Colonna) with the preparatory investigation toward canonization. It seems that the three cardinals made greater use of the Castellano Process than of Raymond of Capua's *Legenda maior*, as "they found in that documentation the depositions of many people who had known Catherine of Siena, and the official authority of the Venice investigation conferred on it some legal status, which was not the case of Raymond's account, the work of a single person written for other persons at their request" (M.-H. Laurent (ed.), "Il Processo Castellano," op. cit., p. xlix).

37. A detailed inventory of papal pronouncements can be found in I. Venchi, "S. Caterina da Siena nel giudizio dei Papi," in *Urbis et orbis*, op. cit., pp. 410–64. R. Rusconi has written that Catherine's canonization provided Dominicans with "a model to offer to the cult and imitation by an increasing number of communities of devout women, who could not become nuns on account of their modest origins and legal impediments" ("Da Costanza al Laterano: La 'calcolata devozione' del ceto mercantile-borghese nell'Italia del Quattrocento," in A. Vauchez (ed.), *Storia dell'Italia religiosa. I. L'antichità e il Medioevo*, Bari, 1993, pp. 529–30). There is no need here to discuss this assertion, all the more so as the meaning of Catherine's canonization for the Dominican order is quite complex.

38. The original Latin text is in *Acta Apostolicae Sedis* 31 (1939), pp. 256–57.

39. Cited previously.

PART I

TEXTUAL CRITICISM

Is the Teaching Found in Her Writings Attributable to Catherine?

The question to be addressed in this first part is the following: is it possible to speak of "Catherine's writings" and therefore of an authentic concept of discretion attributable to Catherine? In other words, is this notion attributable to her own thinking? As was mentioned earlier, there are no autographs by Catherine. Her writings are found in collected manuscripts attributed more or less directly to several of her disciples. For precisely this reason, it is essential to investigate—if only summarily—the complex question of the authenticity of Catherine's writings.

This investigation is divided into four chapters. The purpose of the first is to clarify which writings are definitely attributable to the saint, briefly examining the question whether Catherine knew how to write. The three subsequent chapters address the questions of the composition, transcription, and collection of Catherine's writings, assessing their authenticity. Following the order in which the critical question of authenticity has been raised, the analysis begins with the Letters, moves to the Dialogue, and concludes with the Prayers.

Chapter 1

Textual Criticism of Catherine's Writings

1. INTRODUCTION

The expression "writings of Catherine of Siena," as used here, refers to the whole of the 382 letters comprising the *Letters*, to the *Dialogue* or *Book of Divine Providence*, and to the 26 prayers collectively titled *Prayers*. The *Devout revelation* or *Dialogus brevis*, the author of which remains uncertain, is not included among them and therefore warrants only brief mention at the beginning of this chapter.

2. THE *DEVOUT REVELATION* OR *DIALOGUS BREVIS*

No original version of this writing exists,[1] but there are two known editions: one in Latin and one in the vernacular. The Latin text, titled *Dialogus brevis Sanctae Catherinae Senensis consummatam continens perfectionem*, was first published in 1537 by Marco Civile,[2] who was not only the publisher of this work but also the editor of an older

---

1. See F. Valli, *La "Devota revelazione" o "Dialogus brevis" di santa Caterina da Siena*, Siena, 1928.
2. Valli identified Marco Civile as Marco da Brescia, who, in 1496, published for the first time the Latin version of the *Dialogue*, which had been attributed to Raymond of Capua. (Ibid., pp. 24–26.)

translation.[3] The edition in the vernacular, titled *Una devota revelazione la quale ebbe Sancta Caterina da Siena da Dio di venire a perfectione* ("A devout revelation that Saint Catherine of Siena had from God to come to perfection"), was discovered by Innocenzo Taurisano in codex 1495 at the Riccardian Library in Florence. This vernacular text, which apparently dates back to the fifteenth century, was first published by the same scholar in 1922.[4]

Francesco Valli has shown that both editions come from a single Latin text, which has not been found.[5] The writing was also published in 1707 by Girolamo Gigli in the fourth volume of his edition of Catherine's works; he included it as a "fifth treatise" in addition to the four in the *Dialogue*.[6] Gigli, who claims to have taken it from a Latin exemplar printed in Lyons in 1552,[7] warns that this treatise

3. On this, see the internal and external factors, which Valli lists to show that there was an earlier, now lost, edition. (Ibid., pp. 24–29.)

4. I. Taurisano, "Il piccolo Dialogo della Perfezione," in I. Taurisano (ed.), *Fioretti di S. Caterina da Siena* (1st edn.), Roma, 1922, pp. 155–72. (These pages have not been reproduced in the English translation: *The Little Flowers of Saint Catherine of Siena* (C. Dease tr.), London, 1929.) Innocenzo Taurisano, OP (1877–1960), was prior of the Dominican Convent of Santa Maria sopra Minerva in Rome and the author of many historical studies on the Dominican order and some of its main exponents, such as Dominic, Thomas Aquinas, Catherine of Siena, Beato Angelico, and Savonarola.

5. F. Valli, *La "Devota revelazione*," op. cit., pp. 32–37.

6. *L'Opere di S.Caterina da Siena nuovamente pubblicate da Gerolamo Gigli.* vol. 4: *Il Dialogo della serafica Santa Caterina da Siena, composto in volgare dalla medesima, essendo Lei, mentre dettava ai suoi Scrittori, rapita in singolare eccesso, ed astrazione di mente, diviso in quattro trattati. Opera cavata ora fedelmente dagli antichi testi originali a penna scritti da' Discepoli della Santa a dettatura di Lei; dalla quale scrittura restano corrette di molti considerabili errori le passate divolgazioni. Aggiuntovi ultimamente uno quinto trattato, tolto dalla Libreria Vaticana, e le Orazioni della Santa, con alcuni de' suoi particolari documenti non più stampati. Ed una Scrittura apologetica di Monsig. Raffaelle Maria Filamondo, Vescovo di Stessa, contro alcuni detrattori della Santa. Al Reverendissimo Padre Michel Angelo Tamburini, Preposito Generale della Compagnia di Gesù*, in Siena, nella Stamperia del Pubblico, l'anno 1707. Girolamo Gigli (1660–1722), a learned man from Siena, actively participated in the controversy on language against the Florentine *Accademia della Crusca.*

7. Valli raises doubts on the very existence of the Lyonnaise edition, which Gigli claims to have used for his own version, and instead suggests that, behind Gigli's version, there was a 1554 edition from Leuven, Belgium. (F. Valli, *La "Devota revelazione*," op. cit., p. 7.)

cannot be consistent with the other four, in its style, because it was vulgarized from Latin. This difference in style, however, did not prevent Gigli from attributing the *Dialogus brevis* to Catherine. It would seem, on the contrary, that the stylistic differences between the *Dialogus brevis* and Catherine's other writings go well beyond what is entailed by a simple vulgarization of the original text.[8] Furthermore, this minor work never appears in the earliest collections of Catherine's works and is not mentioned in either the writings of her disciples or the depositions at the Castellano Process. Thus, despite Valli's support for its attribution to Catherine,[9] today most scholars consider the *Dialogus brevis* a presentation of her doctrine authored by one of her disciples.[10]

The uncertain attribution of the *Dialogus brevis* epitomizes one of the thorniest issues regarding Catherine's writings, namely their authenticity. Hence the need to address a series of complex questions that Eugenio Dupré Theseider designates as the "Catherinian problem,"[11] starting with the question whether Catherine knew how to write.

8. J. Hurtaud has emphatically written that, in the *Dialogus brevis*, there is none of the style, color, accent, or devouring flame that one finds in Catherine's *Letters* and *Dialogue*. (J. Hurtaud (ed.), *Le Dialogue de Sainte Catherine de Sienne*, Paris, 1913, p. lxxiv.)

9. F. Valli, *La "Devota revelazione,"* op. cit., pp. 40–52.

10. See, for example, the authoritative view expressed in G. Cavallini, *Caterina da Siena—La verità dell'amore*, op. cit., p. 32, note 42.

11. E. Dupré Theseider, "Il problema critico delle Lettere di santa Caterina da Siena," in *Bullettino dell'Istituto Storico Italiano e Archivio Muratoriano* 49 (1933), pp. 117–278, at p. 250, where the author writes of a "problem" regarding Catherine's letters. The first scholar to have addressed this problem was Robert Fawtier (1885–1966), professor of medieval history and former director of the National Center for Scientific Research (CNRS) in Paris. Fawtier's approach was the subject of criticism by Taurisano and others. See, on this, the useful appendix in A. Curtayne, *Saint Catherine of Siena*, London, 1934, pp. 219–56.

3. DID CATHERINE KNOW HOW TO WRITE?

According to all the hagiographical sources regarding Catherine, she did not write but dictated her works. Raymond of Capua, her confessor and secretary[12] and the author of the most authoritative biography of Catherine,[13] writes:

> She used to dictate those letters of hers with such rapidity, without the slightest pause to take thought, that one would have fancied she was reading out her words from a book lying open before

12. Blessed Raymond of Capua (circa 1330–1399) played a decisive role in the reform of the Dominican order as its master general, which earned him the nickname of "second founder." In 1374, when moving to Siena to be a lector at the local Dominican convent, he became "teacher and director" of both Catherine and her confraternity. He had been in touch with Catherine's confessor, though, already before moving to Siena and had initially been skeptical about the extraordinary phenomena linked to Catherine. But he soon acknowledged their supernatural origin. Infected by the plague while assisting the sick in 1374, he recovered his health through Catherine's intercession. Raymond accompanied Catherine in her many peregrinations. For example, he was himself the celebrant of the Mass in Pisa when, on April 1, 1375, Catherine received the stigmata. He was also with Catherine in Avignon, in 1376, as her interpreter in her conversations with the pope. In March 1378, he obtained for Catherine, from Pope Gregory XI, the authority to negotiate peace with Florence, which was then concluded under Pope Urban VI. Raymond last met Catherine in December 1378, receiving her last letters in February 1380. The day of Catherine's death, while about to leave for the General Chapter in Bologna where he would be elected master general, Raymond heard Catherine's voice that encouraged him and promised him her help. As a principal supporter of Catherine's cult, he described her life in the *Legenda maior*, organized in 1385 a solemn feast day on the occasion of the return of Catherine's head to Siena, and, more generally, worked for the saint's canonization until the end of his days. On Raymond, see the classic H.-M. Cormier, *Le bienheureux Raymonde de Capoue XXIIIe Maître Général de l'Ordre des frères-prêcheurs. Sa vie, ses vertus, son action dans l'Église et dans l'Ordre de Saint Dominique* (2nd edn.), Rome et Paris, 1902. (Cormier was himself a master general of the Dominicans.) See also A. W. Van Ree, "Raymond de Capoue. Éléments biographiques," in *Archivum Fratrum Praedicatorum* 33 (1963), pp. 159–241.

13. Though a work of hagiography according the standards of the time, the *Legenda maior* is meticulous in reflecting what its author had heard, either directly or from witnesses. See T. Centi, "Le 'Leggende' del beato Raimondo di Capua e la critica storica," in *S. Caterina da Siena* 16 (1965, No. 2), pp. 12–17.

her. I myself often saw her dictating at the same time to two different secretaries, two different letters, addressed to two different
persons, and dealing with two different subject-matters; and in the
process neither secretary ever had to wait the fraction of a second
for the dictation he was taking, nor did either of them ever hear
from her anything but what belonged to his own subject-matter
at the moment. When I expressed my astonishment at this I was
told by several who had known her before I did, and who had very
frequently watched while she dictated, that she would sometimes
dictate in this way to three secretaries, and sometimes even to four,
with equal rapidity and sureness of concentration.[14]

According to Raymond of Capua, Catherine learned how to read,
though not without difficulty, yet he does not add that she knew how
to write, and he goes on to list the names of three people who worked
as her secretaries: Stefano di Corrado Maconi,[15] Neri di Landoccio de'
Pagliaresi,[16] and Barduccio di Piero Canigiani.[17]

That Catherine dictated her writings is also confirmed by several depositions from the Castellano Process. Thus, the deposition
by Stefano di Corrado Maconi, a disciple and secretary of the saint,
confirms Raymond of Capua's statements regarding dictation.[18]

---

14. *Life*, pp. 6–7, para. 7.

15. Stefano di Corrado Maconi, a nobleman from Siena, first met Catherine in
1376, becoming one of her secretaries and accompanying her first to Avignon and
then Rome. After Catherine's death, and following her advice, he became a Carthusian
monk and was elected general of his order in 1398. He died in 1424. For a short profile,
see *Letters*, IV, p. 404.

16. Neri di Landoccio de' Pagliaresi, also a nobleman from Siena, was a disciple
and a secretary of Catherine. After her death, he lived as a hermit until his death in
1406. See *Letters*, IV, p. 394.

17. Barduccio di Piero Canigiani, the heir to an ancient family in Florence, probably first met Catherine in 1374, remaining one of her secretaries and faithful followers
until her death, which event he described in detail in a long letter to Sister Catherine
Petriboni. In conformity with Saint Catherine's wish, after her death Barduccio
remained with the Dominicans, but he fell ill pretty soon and died in Siena in 1382. On
Barduccio, see *Letters*, IV, pp. 373–74.

18. See M.-H. Laurent (ed.), "Il Processo Castellano," op. cit., p. 260.

Bartolomeo Dominici, Catherine's confessor,[19] in turn confirms her unique manner of dictating to even two or three secretaries at the same time.[20] Some of the testimonies from the Castellano Process also allude to the miraculous manner in which Catherine supposedly learned not only to read but also to write. For example, Francesco di Vanni Malavolti[21] mentions, in his deposition, the "schools" of the Holy Spirit where Catherine purportedly learned to read and write.[22]

Tommaso di Antonio da Siena, known as "Caffarini,"[23] narrates in his deposition at the Castellano Process[24] and his *Libellus de Supplemento*[25] how Catherine had miraculously learned to write, composing by her own hand a prayer to the Holy Spirit, a few pages of the *Dialogue*, and several letters to her disciples. This seems to find confirmation in letter 272, which is the one containing the framework of the *Dialogue* in embryonic form. According to the final part of the letter, Catherine miraculously learned how to write in the autumn 1377, while she was a guest of the Salimbeni family at Tentennano castle in Rocca d'Orcia.

Several scholars such as Robert Fawtier, though considering letter 272 authentic on the whole,[26] believe that the concluding part was

---

19. Bartolomeo di Domenico (or Bartolomeo Dominici), who had joined the Dominicans at a very young age, since 1368 had been in contact with Catherine, who wrote him several letters (the first one perhaps in 1372). Having become one of Catherine's habitual confessors, he accompanied her to Pisa, Lucca, and Avignon. He saw Catherine again in Rome, a few days before her death. Bartolomeo died in 1415. See *Letters*, IV, p. 374.

20. M.-H. Laurent (ed.), "Il Processo Castellano," op. cit., p. 305.

21. Francesco di Messer Vanni Malavolti, who belonged to one of the most powerful families in Siena, was introduced to Catherine by Neri di Landoccio de' Pagliaresi. Influenced by the saint, he became her disciple and, perhaps, also her occasional secretary. Upon the death of his wife and children, in 1388 he became a monk at Monte Oliveto Maggiore. See *Letters*, IV, pp. 381–82.

22. M.-H. Laurent (ed.), "Il Processo Castellano," op. cit., p. 403.

23. Tommaso di Antonio da Siena, known as "Caffarini," had been in touch with Catherine since 1364 and, after her death, was the chief promoter of her cult. He died in Venice in 1434. See *Letters*, IV, p. 405.

24. M.-H. Laurent (ed.), "Il Processo Castellano," op. cit., pp. 62–63.

25. Thomas Antonii de Senis "Caffarini," *Libellus de Supplemento*, op. cit., pp. 16–17.

26. Fawtier follows Gigli's numbering system, with the consequence that, for him, the letter in question is letter 90.

added by Caffarini, to whom Fawtier attributes the invention of the miraculous event in question.[27] Dupré Theseider, on the other hand, is more cautious. While confirming, in the introduction to his critical edition of the *Letters*, that Catherine "did not know how to write,"[28] he is less categorical in another of his works.[29] This led him to conclude, in a later study, that "there are not, and perhaps there never have been, any autograph writings by Catherine (except for the letter or letters written at Tentennano castle)."[30]

In conclusion, one is left in the realm of possibility: if, on the one hand, it cannot be ruled out that Catherine knew how to write, on the other hand, there are no autograph writings in support of this claim.

4. CONCLUSION

The fact that Catherine dictated her writings does not prove she never learned to write, perhaps toward the end of her life: dictation and ability to write are independent questions from one another. What matters for the purposes of this study is that one can never go back to anything written by Catherine herself: between Catherine and those who read her writings, there is invariably the interposing presence of the amanuenses—with their different levels of learning and training—who were her disciples and to whom the manuscript collections are attributed.

The next three chapters therefore address the question of the role played by these amanuenses and, hence, the authenticity of Catherine's writings. The *Letters* are discussed first, since it was

27. R. Fawtier, *Sainte Catherine de Sienne—Essai de critique des sources*, vol. 2, Paris 1930, pp. 320–28 and 335.

28. E. Dupré Theseider (ed.), *Epistolario di Santa Caterina da Siena*, vol. 1, Roma, 1940, p. xiv. The same assertion is present in an earlier article by the same author: "Il problema critico," op. cit., p. 222.

29. E. Dupré Theseider, "Sono autentiche le Lettere di S. Caterina?" in *Vita Cristiana* 12 (1940), pp. 212–48, at p. 244.

30. E. Dupré Theseider, "Caterina da Siena, santa," op. cit., p. 376.

primarily their study that led several scholars to develop their views on the composition and authenticity of Catherine's writings. It is also appropriate to start from the *Letters*, because it is in the letters that a saint's soul is more immediately reflected, and Catherine's case is not any different: "it is in her letters that one better and more easily learns to know her."[31]

31. F. Weber, "Santa Caterina da Siena vista dalle sue lettere," in *La civiltà cattolica* 98 (1947, No. 2), pp. 236–47, at p. 238.

Chapter 2

Composition and Authenticity of the *Letters*

1. INTRODUCTION

The title "Letters" denotes a collection of 382 letters written between 1370 (but perhaps even earlier) and 1380, the year of Catherine's death, to different categories of addressees: popes, cardinals, other religious, sovereigns, politicians, relatives, friends, people she knew, and even people she had never personally met.

The number of 382 letters was determined by Eugenio Dupré Theseider after discovering at the Palatine Library in Vienna a new manuscript containing them, namely codex 3514, otherwise known as the Vienna Codex (Mo).[1] According to Dupré Theseider, the initial core consists of the 372 letters published by Gigli and Tommaseo,[2] to which one should add the six discovered by Gardner,[3] the two found

---

1. On this codex, see E. Dupré Theseider, "Un codice inedito dell'epistolario di santa Caterina da Siena," in *Bullettino dell'Istituto Storico Italiano e Archivio Muratoriano* 48 (1932), pp. 12–56. On the history of the letters, their composition, and editions, see *Letters*, I, pp. xvi–xxxix.

2. From the 372 letters published by Gigli and Tommaseo, Dupré Theseider eliminates letter 371, as it lacks the usual form and tone of Catherine's letters. Moreover, this letter seems to be always linked, in the various manuscripts, to letter 373. Hence, according to Dupré Theseider, letters 371 and 373 were part of the same text and were jointly sent to Blessed Raymond (E. Dupré Theseider, "Il problema critico," op. cit., pp. 119–20).

3. These letters were published by E. G. Gardner, *Saint Catherine of Siena*, op. cit., pp. 407–22 (Appendix). In this volume, in reality, Gardner published eight letters: the

by Fawtier,[4] and the two identified by Dupré Theseider himself in the Vienna Codex (Mo).[5]

No other manuscript has been found since Dupré Theseider's discovery of the Vienna Codex (Mo). Hence 382 remains the commonly accepted number, which is also the number provided in recent editions of Catherine's letters.

2. ORIGINALS OF THE *LETTERS*

As was noted earlier, the term *original*, when applied to Catherine's writings, does not mean autograph writings but authentic writings, dictated by Catherine to her secretaries.

There are only eight originals of Catherine's letters. Of these, six are in Siena: letters 298, 320, 329, 332, and 319 can be found in manuscript T.III.3 at the Communal Library, while letter 365 can be found at Saint Lucy's church, also in Siena. The seventh original, letter 192, is at the Dominican monastery in Acireale, Sicily. The last original, known as "Letter Fawtier 16,"[6] is at the Oratory of Saint Aloysius Gonzaga's church in Oxford, England.

Of these eight originals, letter 298 was definitely written by Neri di Landoccio de' Pagliaresi, one of Catherine's disciples, as attested by his signature. Identifying the other writers is difficult,[7] though there

---

six he had discovered and two additional ones that had already been published, though only in part.

4. R. Fawtier, "Catheriniana," in *Mélanges d'archéologie et d'histoire* 34 (1914), pp. 3–95.

5. While not discovering any new letter, the historian and filologist Bachisio Raimondo Motzo (1883–1970) has the merit of having reconstructed the integral text of some letters by finding, in Casanatense 292, fragments of letters 322, 356, 328, 336, 321, 334, and 344 (B. R. Motzo, "Alcune lettere di S. Caterina da Siena in parte inedite," in *Bullettino Senese di Storia Patria* 18 (1911), pp. 369–95).

6. This letter is known as "Fawtier 16" because it was discovered by R. Fawtier, who published it in No. 16 of *Catheriniana*, op. cit., pp. 31–32.

7. For a description of the originals and the various theories on who were the writers of the seven unsigned letters, see R. Fawtier, *Sainte Catherine de Sienne—Essai de critique des sources*, vol. 2, op. cit., pp. 15–29.

is support for the proposition that all eight originals were written within the Sienese context. In fact, the six originals that are today in Siena are all addressed to Stefano di Corrado Maconi, the letter in Oxford is addressed to a certain "Messere Jacomo di Viva," and the letter in Acireale is addressed to Neri di Landoccio de' Pagliaresi. At least seven of the eight originals are therefore linked to the inner circle of Catherine's disciples.

3. MANUSCRIPTS OF THE *LETTERS*

Only copies (not originals) of Catherine's letters are contained in the various manuscripts. Of the fifty-five existing manuscripts, twenty-seven alone can be considered true collections of Catherine's letters,[8] even though they do not contain the entire body of the *Letters*. The other twenty-eight contain just a few letters—sometimes only one—included in a miscellany of devout writings.

As to the compilation of these manuscripts, controversy still surrounds the idea that Ser Cristofano di Gano Guidini, a Sienese notary and disciple of Catherine, was responsible for the first collection.[9]

8. This is the list of the manuscripts, with the abbreviations adopted by Fawtier and Dupré Theseider: A Milan, Ambrosiano I.162; B Milan, Braidense AD XIII.34; C Rome, Casanatense 292; F1 Florence, Nazionale II.VIII.5; F2 Florence, Strozziano XXXV.187; F3 Magliabechiano XXXV.199; F4 Florence, Magliabechiano XXXVIII.130; H London, Harleiano 3480; M Modena, SS. Annunziata (now in the archives of the Cathedral); Mo Vienna, Palatino 3514; P1 Florence, Palatino 58; P2 Florence, Palatino 60; P3 Florence, Palatino 57; P4 Florence, Palatino 56; P5 Florence, Palatino 59; Pa Paris, Bibl. Nat., Fonds Ital.1002; R1 Florence, Riccardiano 1678; R2 Florence, Riccardiano 1303; Ro Rome, S. Pantaleo 9; S1 Siena, Comunale, T.III.5; S2 Siena, Comunale, T.II.2; S3 Siena, Comunale, T.II.3; S4 Siena, Comunale, T.II.10; S5 Siena, Comunale, I.IV.14; S6 Siena, Comunale, I.VI.12; T Turin, Bibl. di S.M. il Re Imperatore 155; V Volterra, Guarnacciano 6140. For a detailed description of the manuscripts, see *Letters*, I, pp. 317–44.

9. Cristofano di Gano Guidini was a notary from Siena who, after the plague of 1390 took away from him his wife and six of their seven children, embraced the religious life as an oblate. He died at the end of 1410. He had probably first met Catherine at the beginning of the 1370s. Historians continue debating the role he played in Catherine's circle. For some, he was a secretary; others, instead, think he had a minor

Fawtier contests this idea primarily because Guidini, in his *Memorie* ("Memorial"),[10] does not write about having collected Catherine's letters.[11] Dupré Theseider, on the other hand, does not rule out the existence of a collection by Guidini; he reaches this conclusion on the basis of Caffarini's testimony[12] and deposition at the Castellano Process,[13] which indicates that Guidini apparently collected many of Catherine's letters into two volumes that later became part of Caffarini's collection. According to Dupré Theseider, Guidini's collection underwent a certain degree of transformation, whereby the letters in the collection were arranged in a new order.[14] Whatever the case, there is no trace of the hypothetical Guidini collection unless one is willing to accept Dupré Theseider's opinion that the manuscript he discovered in Vienna is perhaps its filiation, at least in part.[15]

It can nonetheless be supposed that, after Catherine's death and despite the greater consideration given to the *Dialogue* from a doctrinal point of view, several of her disciples may have compiled partial manuscript collections of her letters for private use. The oldest of these collections are probably the Codex Magliabechiano (F4) in Florence[16] and the Codex Casanatense (C) in Rome.[17]

Later on, the addition of more letters resulted in the creation of larger collections intended for dissemination. The long and meticulous analytical task of determining the relations and filiations of

role. In any event, Guidini certainly played an important role with respect to the gathering and transmission of the first collection of Catherine's letters. See *Letters*, IV, p. 379.

10. I. Taurisano, *The Little Flowers*, op. cit., "The Memorial of Ser Cristofano," pp. 92–104.

11. R. Fawtier, *Sainte Catherine de Sienne—Essai de critique des sources*, vol. 2, op. cit., pp. 85–86.

12. Thomas Antonii de Senis "Caffarini," *Libellus de Supplemento*, op. cit., p. 394.

13. M.-H. Laurent (ed.), "Il Processo Castellano," op. cit., p. 73. The same view is expressed by Angelo Salvetti in his deposition (at p. 440).

14. E. Dupré Theseider, "Il problema critico," op. cit., pp. 130–35.

15. Ibid., pp. 135, 140–42, and 145.

16. Codex F4 is a minute collection on paper, while other codices, containing a greater number of letters, are on parchment. This seems to confirm that the latter ones were meant for wide circulation, which was not the case of codex F4. See E. Dupré Theseider, "Sono autentiche," op. cit., p. 222.

17. E. Dupré Theseider, "Il problema critico," op. cit., p. 239.

the most important manuscripts has led some scholars to group the codices into three families. They are distinguished by the names of their compilers, all of whom were disciples of Catherine and the first two of whom were also her secretaries: Stefano di Corrado Maconi, Neri di Landoccio de' Pagliaresi, and Caffarini. The first two collections seem to have been independent of one another. Caffarini, who compiled his collection later, appears to have taken much of his material from Pagliaresi's collection and very little from Maconi's.[18]

In addition to these three groups of manuscripts, there is also a shorter collection of great importance because it is believed to have been compiled by Barduccio di Piero Canigiani, who was both a disciple and a secretary of Catherine. This is the Casanatense 292 (C) manuscript, discovered by Gardner. This codex, which includes an old copy of the *Dialogue* in its first part, contains forty-seven letters arranged in an irregular and nonhierarchical manner, which gives reason to believe that it may be one of the oldest collections.

Having briefly summarized the origins of the manuscript collections, the question remains of ascertaining the criteria that led to the formation of the *Letters*.

4. COMPOSITION OF THE *LETTERS*

(i) The Work of the Copyists

Letter 373, which is addressed to Raymond of Capua and considered Catherine's "spiritual will," contains the following passage:

> I also ask you and Frate Bartolomeo and Frate Tommaso and the
> master to take care of the book and any other writing of mine

---

18. Fawtier and Dupré Theseider adopted different approaches to establish connections between manuscripts. Fawtier insisted on numeric concordance (for example, letter 39 can be found in codices Mo, S5, S6): R. Fawtier, *Sainte Catherine de Sienne— Essai de critique des sources*, vol. 2, op. cit., pp. 81–108. Dupré Theseider, instead, privileged the order in which letters follow one another in the codices: E. Dupré Theseider, "Il problema critico," op. cit., pp. 126–29.

you may find. You, together with Messere Tommaso, do with them whatever you see would be most to God's honor.[19]

Dupré Theseider sees the five individuals named in this excerpt as a sort of small committee for the revision of the official edition of Catherine's works; its authoritativeness would come from the fact that its members were selected by Catherine herself.[20] While the existence of this "revision committee" is only hypothetical, it is clear that Catherine's letters underwent certain mutilations when they were recopied into the manuscript collections intended for dissemination. This gives reason to believe that her disciples carried out some degree of preliminary revision.

The first type of cut left traces of the mutilations it caused. For example, the irritating "*et caetera*" occasionally interrupts the text of the letters, almost always near the final section of the text, which clearly indicates a mutilation. Cuts of another type occur toward the end of the letters, but these were done without leaving any trace. Scholars have discovered them by comparing, wherever possible, the complete (and therefore longer) letters contained in certain codices with those same letters (of shorter length) in other codices.

A clear example of this second type of cut becomes evident if one compares two codices that share some of the same letters: the Codex Magliabechiano F4 in Florence and the Vienna Codex (Mo), which scholars regard as having been written by the same hand, namely that of Neri di Landoccio de' Pagliaresi.[21] The comparison

19. *Letters*, IV, p. 369 (*Lettere*, V, p. 291).

20. On the five persons mentioned in letter 373, E. Dupré Theseider writes: "Probably, the first is Giovanni Tantucci, master of theology, and the second is Tommaso Petra, apostolic protonotary. The others are Father Raymond of Capua, the saint's confessor; Father Bartolomeo Dominici, then cardinal; Father Tommaso Caffarini" ("Un codice inedito," op. cit., pp. 12–56, at p. 31).

21. R. Fawtier saw Pagliaresi's hand in codex F4 (*Sainte Catherine de Sienne—Essai de critique des sources*, vol. 2, op. cit., p. 119, note 3). E. Dupré Theseider added that Pagliaresi had written not only codex F4 but also the greater part of the Vienna Codex (Mo) ("Un codice inedito," op. cit., pp. 23–24).

shows Pagliaresi, Catherine's disciple and secretary, at work as a "censor": it appears that he copied the letters from the originals in integral form, for his own private remembrance, in the short Codex Magliabechiano, whereas he transcribed them in abbreviated form in the long manuscript of the Vienna Codex (Mo) that was intended for dissemination.[22] This confirms that, while the letters in the oldest and shortest collections—such as the Codex Magliabechiano F4 in Florence and the Codex Casanatense (C) in Rome—were almost always copied from the originals in integral form, the same did not occur when efforts began to coordinate the material from the letters for dissemination and moral instruction.

Hence the obvious question: why did the copyists make these cuts? In Fawtier's opinion, the letters were deliberately mutilated by Catherine's disciples to remove anything that might have been an obstacle to her canonization. The primary culprit behind this plot would have been Caffarini, the foremost promoter of devotion to Catherine and the first to undertake the challenge of forming an official collection of the letters.[23] Yet, Fawtier's conjecture is not plausible because in many cases Caffarini did not cover the trail of his mutilations, which does not fit with the theory of a prearranged plot. Furthermore, as Dupré Theseider shows,[24] the cuts were the result of individual initiatives, and this reduces the likelihood of a pious group of conspirators trying to present Catherine as someone "interested solely in the salvation of souls and the good of the Church."[25] Finally, the fact that the mutilations—usually found toward the end of the letters—primarily affect the closing and parts of the text containing family or confidential news and allusions to personal matters seems to indicate that the reason for these mutilations is quite different.

22. E. Dupré Theseider, "Sono autentiche," op. cit., pp. 230–32.
23. R. Fawtier, *Sainte Catherine de Sienne—Essai de critique des sources*, vol. 2, op. cit., pp. 122–24.
24. E. Dupré Theseider, "Sono autentiche," op. cit., p. 224.
25. R. Fawtier, *Sainte Catherine de Sienne—Essai de critique des sources*, vol. 2, op. cit., p. 123.

Dupré Theseider also points out that Catherine's disciples valued the letters above all as devout and inspired compositions. In copying the letters into large collections intended for the moral instruction of the faithful, the copyists sought to eliminate those parts in which Catherine discussed the contingent realities of her time and place, which they considered to be of interest only to the immediate circle of the letters' addressees.[26] This explanation is convincing and certainly preferable to the one advanced by Fawtier.

(ii) The Work of the Secretaries

If the influence of the secretaries in the process of copying the various collections is a complex question, it is all the more complicated to determine the role they played in the composition of Catherine's writings, particularly the letters.

Dupré Theseider considers it likely that Catherine's style, and perhaps even her thoughts, may have been altered. This supposition appears to be supported by the fact that the text of the letters was handed down in an almost "courtly" form, which is to say that the vernacular forms in which Catherine almost certainly expressed herself were heavily attenuated.[27]

Dupré Theseider does not believe it possible, furthermore, that the secretaries took all of the letters down in writing from dictation, from the first word to the last. A rather curious episode mentioned by Francesco di Vanni Malavolti in his deposition at the Castellano Process sheds some light on this point. One day, Catherine was dictating three different letters at the same time to the three secretaries, one of whom was Malavolti. All three amanuenses wrote down certain phrases that the saint had dictated to only one of them. When they realized it, they were upset about the error; however, Catherine urged them to wait until the dictation was over. In fact, once the

26. E. Dupré Theseider, "Un codice inedito," op. cit., p. 32.
27. E. Dupré Theseider (ed.), *Epistolario di Santa Caterina da Siena*, vol. 1, op. cit., p. xiv.

dictation had ended, each of the secretaries reread his own letter and discovered that those phrases fit perfectly in the text.[28] Fawtier regards this story as the evidence of inaccuracies in Malavolti's deposition.[29] Dupré Theseider, on the other hand, considers it a clear and ingenuous description of the dictation, in the sense that the state of ecstasy into which the saint often lapsed during dictation caused her to lose control over the precision of the dictation and that, since Catherine's speech was hardly intelligible and rapid while in the throes of ecstasy, the amanuenses ended up with just a skeletal draft that they would later use to expand the text of the letter.[30] This would explain why Catherine's style, while "unmistakably her own" (at least in certain expressions and phrases), "is not inimitable."[31]

The fact is that Dupré Theseider's suppositions, though ingenious, remain purely hypothetical and indeed have not been accepted by all other scholars. For example, Alvaro Grion has expressed the opposite view: there is no document indicating that Catherine dictated the skeleton of her letters, and the testimonies of all the hagiographers instead concur on direct dictation.[32] Other scholars think it is difficult to maintain that the saint dictated her letters in a hardly intelligible manner since all of the witnesses attest that her dictation was clear and precise, most notably during her ecstasies.[33]

Evidence of mediation by her disciples in shaping Catherine's writings nonetheless remains, leading Dupré Theseider to conclude that "the possibility, if not the certitude, of alterations of her text—and therefore of her thought, as any written text is an eminently spiritual fact—is always present, and we have to accept this."[34]

---

28. M.-H. Laurent (ed.), "Il Processo Castellano," op. cit., pp. 403–4.

29. R. Fawtier, *Sainte Catherine de Sienne—Essai de critique des sources*, vol. 2, op. cit., p. 5.

30. E. Dupré Theseider, "Il problema critico," op. cit., pp. 226–27.

31. E. Dupré Theseider, "Sono autentiche," op. cit., p. 240.

32. A. Grion, *Santa Caterina da Siena. Dottrina e fonti*, Brescia, 1953, pp. 163–64.

33. Among the others, see T. Centi, "Genesi dell'epistolario di Santa Caterina da Siena," in *Archivum Fratrum Praedicatorum* 18 (1947), pp. 285–92, at pp. 290–91.

34. E. Dupré Theseider, "Sono autentiche," op. cit., pp. 241–42.

(iii) The Question of Authenticity

The secretaries' influence on the composition of the letters entails the question of their authenticity. This issue was first put forth by Robert Fawtier, whose interest in Catherine and her works dates back to 1911.[35]

In 1914, Fawtier published several of the saint's unedited letters and letter fragments taken from various manuscripts.[36] He then followed this up, in 1921, with the first critical investigation of the sources of Catherine's writings.[37] It was in this volume from 1921 that Fawtier advanced his theory that Catherine's letters had been manipulated by her disciples—starting with Caffarini, whom Fawtier dubbed the "primary editor"—for the purpose of obtaining her canonization.[38] He changed his mind, however, ten years later in the second volume of the same work,[39] declaring all of Catherine's letters authentic except for one whole letter and the closing of another.[40]

Fawtier's studies led to a reaction by other scholars. In 1928, the Istituto Storico Italiano per il Medio Evo (the "Italian Historical Institute for the Middle Ages") entrusted Eugenio Dupré Theseider with the task of preparing a critical edition of the *Letters*. The first volume came out in 1940 and has regrettably remained the only one to date. (Upon Dupré Theseider's death in 1975, the charge of continuing his work was entrusted to Antonio Volpato at Roma Tre University. On the basis of his own research, Volpato began to make corrections to the first volume of Dupré Theseider's edition.)[41]

---

35. R. Fawtier, *Sainte Catherine de Sienne—Essai de critique des sources*, vol. 2, op. cit., p. vii.

36. R. Fawtier, "Catheriniana," op. cit., pp. 3–95.

37. R. Fawtier, *Sainte Catherine de Sienne—Essai de critique des sources*, vol. 1, Paris, 1921.

38. Ibid., p. xii.

39. Ibid., vol. 2, op. cit., pp. 321–35.

40. The letters in question are letter 273 and the "post-scriptum" of letter 272. (In Fawtier, they are letters 97 and 90, respectively: ibid., pp. 321–30 and 335.)

41. Volpato's edition is not yet available in print, but the text of his edition is reflected in the CD-ROM containing Catherine's writings: Santa Caterina da Siena,

From the conclusions reached by both Fawtier—in his second volume on Catherine's writings[42]—and Dupré Theseider, it is evident that the two scholars agreed in their acknowledgment of the authenticity of the *Letters*, with the exception of two letters that were primarily contested by Fawtier: letter 272, in the concluding part of the text, and letter 273. Fawtier maintained that the concluding part of letter 272 (in which Catherine narrates to Raymond of Capua how she miraculously learned to write, and whose authenticity had already been questioned by Hurtaud)[43] was added later by Caffarini. This proposition seems to be supported by the fact that letter 272 is contained in only those more recent manuscripts that, according to Fawtier, were written under the influence of Caffarini.[44]

Dupré Theseider instead contended that letter 272 can be found in its entirety, including its postscript, in the first part of the Vienna Codex (Mo), which he believed was written before 1389, a decade before Raymond of Capua's death.[45] According to Dupré Theseider, Fawtier had rejected the closing of the letter in question because he ultimately did not accept the "miracle" of her ability to write, whereas Dupré Theseider did not consider these suspicions sufficient to remove letter 272—or, rather, its closing—from the category of authentic letters.[46] On the other hand, the Italian scholar still harbored some doubt regarding its authenticity, though for reasons

---

Opera Omnia. Testi e Concordanze (F. Sbaffoni, ed.), Pistoia, 2002. Volpato's corrections to the edition by Dupré Theseider were obtained and used by S. Noffke in her English edition of Catherine's letters. (See what she writes in the introduction to *Letters*, I, p. xxxv, note 44.)

42. R. Fawtier, *Sainte Catherine de Sienne—Essai de critique des sources*, vol. 2, op. cit.

43. J. Hurtaud (ed.), *Le Dialogue de Sainte Catherine de Sienne*, Paris, 1913 (reprint 1976), vol. 1, p. xliv.

44. R. Fawtier, *Sainte Catherine de Sienne—Essai de critique des sources*, vol. 2, op.cit., pp. 321–28.

45. E. Dupré Theseider, "Sulla composizione del *Dialogo* di santa Caterina da Siena," in *Giornale Storico della Letteratura Italiana* 16 (1941), pp. 161–202, at p. 168, note 1.

46. E. Dupré Theseider, "Sono autentiche," op. cit., p. 244.

different from Fawtier's. In a subsequent article,[47] Dupré Theseider neither denied nor accepted the authenticity of letter 272 in its entirety.

Dupré Theseider's position is much clearer regarding letter 273, which contains an account of the execution of a young man whom Catherine does not name but whom Caffarini identifies as Nicolò di Toldo, who was executed in Siena for political reasons, probably in 1375. Fawtier rejected the authenticity of the letter in question primarily because, in his opinion, Catherine was not in Siena at that time: she had been staying in Pisa for most of 1375.[48] Dupré Theseider, to the contrary, after having examined both the content and style of letter 273, declared that "there is nothing imaginable that is more authentically Catherinian."[49]

5. CONCLUSION

In conclusion, both Fawtier and Dupré Theseider acknowledge that the *Letters* as a whole, though not autographical, are "substantially authentic."[50] In other words, despite the doubts on the postscript of letter 272 and the whole text of letter 273, "the entire body of correspondence comes with considerable authenticity guarantees that are quite exceptional for documents of this nature and time."[51]

47. E. Dupré Theseider, "Sulla composizione del *Dialogo*," op. cit., p. 168.

48. R. Fawtier, *Sainte Catherine de Sienne—Essai de critique des sources*, vol. 2, op. cit., pp. 328–30.

49. E. Dupré Theseider, "Sono autentiche," op. cit., pp. 246–47.

50. Ibid., p. 221.

51. R. Fawtier, *Sainte Catherine de Sienne—Essai de critique des sources*, vol. 2, op. cit., p. 319. Likewise, S. Noffke has remarked: "The linguistic evidence, I believe, establishes beyond a doubt that there can be only a single author of these texts . . . Catherine herself" (*Letters*, I, p. xlvii).

Chapter 3

Composition and Authenticity
of the *Dialogue*

1. INTRODUCTION

The *Dialogue* or *Book of Divine Providence* is generally regarded as Catherine's greatest mystical work, reflecting the spiritual maturity of her thought. According to Fawtier, it may be considered "the essential wellspring from which one must draw to understand the saint."[1]

This work did not have a title during Catherine's lifetime. In letter 373, she refers to it simply as "the book" or "my book" (as in letter 365).[2] Her disciples, too, refer to it as "the book." Raymond of Capua, in talking about Stefano Maconi, notes that "he was one of Catherine's secretaries, and took his share in writing the letters she dictated and the *Book* she composed."[3] In talking about Neri di Landoccio de' Pagliaresi, Raymond states that he was "one of Catherine's secretaries for the writing of her letters and of her *Book*, the other two being Stephen and Barduccio."[4] Cristofano di Gano Guidini writes in his Memorial:

---

1. R. Fawtier, *Sainte Catherine de Sienne—Essai de critique des sources*, vol. 2, op. cit., p. 351.
2. "I sent word to the countess asking for my book." *Letters*, III, p. 137 (*Lettere*, V, p. 257).
3. *Life*, p. 317, para. 342.
4. Ibid., p. 318, para. 343.

This servant of Christ made another notable thing; namely a book which is of the size of a missal; she made it all when she was in an ecstasy, having lost all corporal sense except the power of speech. God the Father spoke to her, and she replied and questioned, and she herself repeated the words which she said to Him; and her questions and all these words were in the vulgar tongue.... This book was thus inscribed: *Book of divine doctrine given by the Person of God the Father speaking to the soul of the glorious and holy virgin, Catherine of Siena, of the habit of penance of the Order of Preachers, and dictated by her in the vulgar tongue; she being in ecstasy, hearing actually and before many persons what God said to her interiorly.*[5]

By writing "this book was thus inscribed," Guidini confirms that a title was only given to the book at a later stage. Actually, the book has had various titles since Catherine's death: *A Book* or *Dialogue* or *Treatise of Divine Providence*, *The Book of Divine Revelation*, *Revelations*, *The Book* or *Dialogue of Divine Doctrine*, and, more frequently, *The Dialogue of Divine Providence*. Today, the work is usually called the *Dialogue*.

2. TIME AND MANNER OF THE *DIALOGUE*'S COMPOSITION

Raymond of Capua mentions two defining moments in the composition of the *Dialogue*. The first one is the vision on which the Book was based:

about two years before her death, God poured so abundant a light of truth into her mind that she felt compelled, in her turn, to pass it on to others in written form. She requested her secretaries, therefore, as already described, whenever they observed

---

5. I. Taurisano, *The Little Flowers*, op. cit., p. 100.

that she was rapt in ecstasy, to be alert to take down whatever they should hear her say.[6]

The second moment is when it was drafted. Raymond of Capua writes that, once she had completed her mission in Florence and the peace accords had been made public, Catherine returned to Siena, where "she became engrossed in the composition of that *Book* of hers which she had already begun to dictate, in her native vernacular, under the inspiration of the Holy Spirit."[7]

Having returned to Siena, Catherine seems to have dedicated herself to the dictation of the book until Urban VI called her to Rome. Raymond of Capua does not imply that the work was completed before her departure for Rome, but that it had been composed in a short time ("*brevi tempore*"):

It was in this way that, in a brief space of time, a certain *Book* was compiled, containing a *Dialogue* between a Soul and the Lord. The Soul presented four petitions to the Lord; he replied to them, and furthermore instructed the Soul concerning a variety of truths of momentous significance.[8]

Additional information can be found in the *Letters*. In letter 365, written in Florence and addressed to Stefano Maconi before June 23, 1378, Catherine asks for her "book" from Countess Bandecca Salimbeni. Having left Florence in the summer 1378, Catherine writes from Siena to Francesco di Pipino, a tailor, in August of that same year: "Give Francesco [Malavolti?] the book...because I want to write something in it."[9]

---

6. *Life*, p. 324, para. 349.
7. Ibid., p. 309, para. 332.
8. Ibid., pp. 324–25, para. 349.
9. This passage belongs to the appendix to letter 179, discovered and published by R. Fawtier, "Catheriniana," op. cit., and republished in E. Dupré Theseider, "Un codice inedito," op. cit., p. 52.

These passages indicate that, when Catherine left Florence for Siena, the work was either completed or at least far enough along to be called a book. Yet Catherine did not consider it finished, because she intended to write something else in it.

Another important date emerges from two manuscripts of the *Dialogue* containing an *explicit* that labels the *Dialogue* as done (*"facto et compilato"*) "in the year of our Lord MCCCLXXVIII in the month of October."[10] While the date of October 1378 seems relatively certain for its completion, there has been extensive debate about the starting date of the work. This has in turn led to various theories about the composition time frame.

Hurtaud makes an astonishing conjecture. Interpreting too literally the *"brevi tempore"* from Raymond of Capua's *Legenda maior*, he writes in the introduction to his French translation of the *Dialogue* that Catherine dictated the entire book while in ecstasy in just five days: from October 9 to 13, 1378.[11] Fawtier's response, which is one among many reactions to Hurtaud's conjecture, is compelling. On the basis of letter 272, which he believes contains the vision giving rise to the *Dialogue* and dates back to October 1377, Fawtier asserts that Catherine began dictating the book in Advent 1377, while she was a guest of the Salimbeni family at Tentennano castle near Rocca d'Orcia, and that she completed it in October 1378 in Siena.[12] This suggestion is also supported by the previously cited letters showing that the book may already have been referred to as such before summer 1378, though Catherine did not consider it completed insofar as she wished to introduce additions or changes.

Dupré Theseider essentially agrees with Fawtier on this. He believes that, since the *Dialogue* makes no reference to the schism, the work must have been completed before news of it reached Catherine, which was in September 1378.[13] Giuliana Cavallini also supports this idea,

---

10. The manuscripts are T.II.9 and I.VI.13 of the Communal Library in Siena.

11. J. Hurtaud (ed.), *Le Dialogue de Sainte Catherine de Sienne*, op. cit., pp. xxxv–li.

12. R. Fawtier, *Sainte Catherine de Sienne—Essai de critique des sources*, vol. 2, op. cit., pp. 343–49.

13. E. Dupré Theseider, "Sulla composizione del *Dialogo*," op. cit., p. 167.

setting the start date of the composition between December 1377 and spring 1378, and the date of completion sometime between August and October 1378. A time span of ten or eleven months would not conflict with the external facts and can be reconciled with Raymond of Capua's *"brevi tempore,"* if the vastness and depth of the subject matter are taken into account.[14]

In summary, the theory of a composition process for the book lasting several months seems to be closer to reality. Scholars are in nearly unanimous agreement that the *Dialogue* was not composed in a few days but rather over a relatively extended period of time, developing from and around an essential core that can be identified in some of the letters, particularly letter 272.

The next question, which is strictly related to the question of the time frame, is the manner of composition of the *Dialogue*. In this regard, Raymond of Capua's testimony describing Catherine's state of ecstasy while dictating is quite explicit:

> There was one thing strange and almost paradoxical about her dictation at these moments. On the one hand, she never dictated save when she was rapt out of herself and altogether cut off from the world of the senses; she saw nothing, heard nothing, smelled nothing, tasted nothing, felt nothing by her sense of touch. And yet, whilst in that state of abstraction from the world of sense, she dictated her *Book* in audible speech. This was the Lord's work, making clear to us that the volume was not composed by mere natural power, but by virtue of a charism of the Holy Spirit.[15]

Several of Catherine's disciples gave similar testimony at the Castellano Process, namely Caffarini, Bartolomeo Dominici, and Francesco Malavolti.[16] Furthermore, even Cristofano di Gano Guidini

---

14. *Dialogo*, pp. xxix–xxx.
15. *Life*, pp. 309–10, para. 332.
16. M.-H. Laurent (ed.), "Il Processo Castellano," op. cit., pp. 98, 305, and 401.

writes in his Memorial about the manner in which the book was composed, stating how it was dictated by Catherine "when she was in an ecstasy, having lost all corporal sense except the power of speech."[17] These testimonies have led several scholars, including Hurtaud, to suppose that the saint dictated the *Dialogue* while in ecstasy.[18] Against this idea, other scholars have instead written of "post-ecstatic" dictation: Catherine would have transmitted whatever her memory had retained of the exchanges with God once she came out of ecstasy.[19]

Fawtier, too, believes that "not everything was dictated while she was in ecstasy or that, after her ecstasies, the saint herself might have critically reviewed the notes taken by her secretaries."[20] Dupré Theseider is in favor of a compromise solution. In his opinion, the *Dialogue* was first conceived upon Catherine's vision at Tentennano castle in October 1377, which she describes to Raymond of Capua in letter 272. Dupré Theseider then adds that the memory of that vision did not abandon her and acted

> as the core for many other memories, deriving from similar visions, and for many observations made at different times in her life, for mystical or moral meditations on the life of man or the Church, on redemption, the Eucharistic doctrine, Trinity, Incarnation, satisfaction, on the mysteries of life and death. This leads to her great work, to which Catherine entrusts the best of her mystical experience.[21]

Essentially, Dupré Theseider maintains that, while the *Dialogue* was conceived in a vision, it would nonetheless become the fruit of such

---

17. I. Taurisano, *The Little Flowers*, op. cit., p. 100.

18. In his introduction to the French edition of the *Dialogue*, J. Hurtaud wrote that Catherine dictated the whole book in a state of ecstasy (*Le Dialogue de Sainte Catherine de Sienne*, op. cit., p. xxxi).

19. Among these scholars, see A. Lemonnyer, *Notre vie spirituelle à l'école de Sainte Catherine de Sienne*, Paris, 1934 (reprint 2009), p. 9.

20. R. Fawtier and L. Canet, *La double experience de Catherine Benincasa (sainte Catherine de Sienne)*, Paris, 1948, p. 187.

21. E. Dupré Theseider, "Sulla composizione del *Dialogo*," op. cit., p. 198.

a long and patient labor process that Catherine ultimately composed the work of her maturity from materials that had already existed. This is a plausible theory, especially if one considers that a large portion of the material contained in the *Dialogue* can be found, however scattered, in the *Letters*.

3. *DIALOGUE'S* RELATION TO THE *LETTERS*

What is the relationship between the *Dialogue* and the *Letters*? In answering this question, as has already been hinted earlier, some scholars regard letter 272 as a draft or first outline of the book, while others consider it a summary. Fawtier limits himself to a brief allusion to the question at hand, simply stating that "there is letter 90, which contains the outline of the *Dialogue*."[22] Hurtaud, on the other hand, considers the question at greater length and highlights how the relationship between the *Dialogue* and letter 272 goes down to the tiniest details. According to this scholar, "in the letter and the Book, one is in the presence of a single and perfectly identical fact": the *Dialogue* and the letter in question can even be formally reconciled because they contain "the same solution formulated in the same words."[23] Having written this, however, Hurtaud does not carry his analysis all the way through.

The credit for beginning a comparative analysis of the *Dialogue* and the *Letters* is due to Dupré Theseider, who made use not only of his expertise in philology and stylistics but also of his extensive knowledge of the studies on Catherine. After an incisive analysis of letter 272, which in his opinion contains a summary of the *Dialogue*

---

22. R. Fawtier, *Sainte Catherine de Sienne—Essai de critique des sources*, vol. 2, op. cit., p. 347. As was noted earlier, Fawtier adopts Gigli's numbering of the letters, with the consequence that, when he refers to letter 90, he refers to the letter that, in Tommaseo's numbering, is letter 272.

23. J. Hurtaud (ed.), *Le Dialogue de Sainte Catherine de Sienne*, op. cit., pp. xxxviii and xlii.

with parallel passages and the four petitions, and after a comparative analysis of the *Dialogue* and the letter in question on the basis of the double-column method, he demonstrates that, in the book, Catherine "copied herself," reproducing in the *Dialogue*, almost in its entirety, the idea of the vision she had experienced in October 1377 and communicated to Raymond of Capua in letter 272, adapting it to the general layout developed in the *Dialogue*.[24] Furthermore, the content from the mystical parts of letters 64 and 65 (addressed to William Flete and Daniella d'Orvieto, respectively) can be found in chapters 98 to 104 of the *Dialogue*. Therefore, in letters 64 and 65 on the one hand, and 272 on the other, there were probably two texts, composed before the *Dialogue*, which would later be amended and inserted in it through a typical process of interpolation. "The opposite theory, namely that those letters derive from the *Dialogue*, seems inadmissible: it would be impossible to understand either its mechanism or its finality."[25]

Who was responsible for elaborating on the text of those letters when they were inserted in the *Dialogue*, intelligently and appropriately adapting them to its peculiarities? Dupré Theseider concludes that Catherine herself, or one of her disciples acting under her control, took the material from those letters and used it in the book. Hence there is only one possible explanation for the fidelity with which the *Dialogue* integrates the passages from letter 272:

Catherine...retains one by one the words of letter 272 because she considers them, in a way, to be consecrated by the exceptional circumstances under which she dictated them. They are the work of "revelation," reflecting her dialogue with God; indeed, they were mostly the words of God, hence true "authority."[26]

24. E. Dupré Theseider, "Sulla composizione del *Dialogo*," op. cit., pp. 169–88.
25. Ibid., p. 197.
26. Ibid., p. 200.

Regrettably, Dupré Theseider limited his comparative analysis to examining only those letters in which the themes and images of the book predominantly recur. Consequently, the question of what portion of the letters was integrated into the *Dialogue* still awaits investigation by some scholar of good will and proven competency.

4. MANUSCRIPTS AND LATIN TRANSLATIONS

Cristofano di Gano Guidini writes in his Memorial, with regard to the composition of the *Dialogue*, that Catherine spoke and someone would write down: "at one time Ser Barduccio, at another the said Donno Stefano, at another Neri di Landoccio. When we hear this it seems incredible, but to those who listened and wrote it does not seem so, and I am of the number."[27]

Raymond of Capua confirms that the three amanuenses for the *Dialogue* were Barduccio di Piero Canigiani, Stefano di Corrado Maconi, and Neri di Landoccio de' Pagliaresi.[28] In his testimony at the Castellano Process, Stefano di Corrado Maconi personally declares that he wrote down part of the book.[29] However, the original manuscript written by these three disciples has been lost, and none of the codices available has the qualities of an original. This is also true of codex T.II.9 at the Communal Library in Siena, which had long been theorized to be the original copy of the *Dialogue*. Matilde Fiorilli dismantled this theory by demonstrating how it was unfounded.[30] Other scholars followed suit.

The *Dialogue* can therefore be reconstructed on the basis of the oldest manuscripts, comparing the latter with the early, and

---

27. I. Taurisano, *The Little Flowers*, op. cit., p. 100.

28. *Life*, p. 318, para. 343.

29. M.-H. Laurent (ed.), "Il Processo Castellano," op. cit., pp. 263–64.

30. Santa Caterina da Siena, *Libro della divina dottrina, volgarmente detto Dialogo della Divina Provvidenza* (M. Fiorilli, ed.), Bari, 1912, p. 417.

authoritative, Latin translations. In fact, Catherine's disciples immediately recognized the need to translate the *Dialogue* into Latin to
ensure wider circulation. The first person to confront this task seems
to have been Guidini, as he himself explains:

> And because the said book is for the vulgar, and those who know
> Latin and are instructed do not so willingly read the things meant
> for the masses as things meant for the lettered, both for myself
> and for the use of my neighbour I set to translate it into Latin
> exactly according to the text, adding nothing. I endeavoured to
> do it as well as I could, and employed several years with joy in the
> work, translating now one passage, now another.[31]

Raymond of Capua, too, probably intended to translate the book into
Latin but only managed to translate the first five chapters before his
death in 1399. It was finally Stefano Maconi who completed a translation of the *Dialogue*, as attested by an *ex libris* of codex AD.IX.35 at
the Brera Library in Milan.[32]

Among the manuscripts, the oldest codices of the *Dialogue* appear
to be codex 292 at the Casanatense Library in Rome, codex T.II.9
at the Communal Library in Siena, and codex T.6.5 at the Estense
Library in Modena. A common feature of all three codices is that the
text is not divided into chapters. Since they were compiled before
the introduction of such divisions, these manuscripts seem to be the
most faithful to the original, even though the codex at the Estense
Library may hastily have been copied, and Cavallini considers it the
"work of someone transcribing by sight with no understanding of the
meaning of the text."[33]

The most authoritative of the three codices appears to be the
codex (C) at the Casanatense Library, which had been relatively

---

31. I. Taurisano, *The Little Flowers*, op. cit., pp. 100–101.

32. See Santa Caterina da Siena, *Dialogo della Divina Provvidenza* (2nd edn.,
I. Taurisano), Roma, 1947, pp. xxvii–xxviii.

33. *Dialogo*, p. xlv, note 37.

unknown and hardly studied until Gardner brought it to the attention of other scholars.[34] Motzo was the first to study it, primarily on account of the letters it contained. Later, upon a more thorough critical examination, he determined that the manuscript of the *Dialogue* contained in the Casanatense (C) is the closest to the original: it is a copy made by Barduccio di Piero Canigiani, one of the three amanuenses, for his private use. Motzo added that the collection of the letters found in the Casanatense (C) is important for its dating and attribution. One of the letters is addressed to "*Piero Canigiani in Fiorenze, patri meo secundum carnem*" ("Piero Canigiani in Florence, my father according to the flesh"). Another has the following heading "*A messere Ristoro Canigiani da Fiorenze, germano meo secundum carnem*" ("To Sir Ristoro Canigiani of Florence, my brother according to the flesh"). The writer is therefore Barduccio Canigiani, son of Piero and brother of Ristoro. Barduccio was Catherine's last disciple and died in Siena in 1382. Hence, if it is likely that codex (C) was compiled by Barduccio Canigiani during his stay in Rome, which was sometime between 1378 and 1381, it must have been completed before December 8, 1382, the date of Barduccio's death.

In Motzo's judgment, one of the peculiarities supporting the idea of a more direct derivation of the Casanatense (C) from the original is the systematic elimination of the pronoun "me" whenever it was connected to the expression "God and man" in the chapters discussing the Eucharistic mystery. This would seem to be the result of the revisions to her writings that Catherine had recommended in her last letter to Raymond of Capua (which is letter 373): "me" would have seemed inappropriate to the editors in reference to the Eternal Father. Motzo observes that this correction is not found in any other manuscript.[35]

---

34. E. G. Gardner, *Saint Catherine of Siena*, op. cit., pp. 418–22.
35. See the extensive analysis coming to this conclusion in B. R. Motzo, "Per un'edizione critica delle opere di S. Caterina da Siena," op. cit., pp. 111–41.

Other indications providing reason to believe that the Casanatense (C) is closer to the original include the absence of interpolations clarifying difficult passages (interpolations that can instead be found in other manuscripts) and less accurate scriptural citations, which are perhaps closer to citations from memory than to the corrected biblical citations found in the other codices. These are some of the reasons that Cavallini provides for basing her critical edition of the *Dialogue* (which is the standard one in use today) on the Casanatense codex,[36] though she admits having collated this manuscript with other codices such as T.II.9 at the Communal Library in Siena and T.6.5 at the Estense Library in Modena.[37]

One of the merits of Cavallini's edition is that it has brought back to light the original structure of the *Dialogue*.

5. STRUCTURE OF THE *DIALOGUE*

It is likely that Catherine's dictation was in the form of continuous narration. This is confirmed by the older codices, such as the Casanatense and the Estense T.6.5, in which the divisions of the dictation are indicated only by an initial capital letter or a new paragraph mark. Scholars agree that the work was first divided into chapters by the saint's disciples, perhaps with the aim of making it easier to read. Codex T.II.9 at the Communal Library in Siena seems to have been the first one to be divided into chapters (for a total of 167). This division was not original but added in the margins at some point after its redaction, along with rubrics indicating the topic of each chapter.[38]

---

36. *Dialogo*, p. xlii. Cavallini based on this manuscript both of her editions of the *Dialogue*, the first one dating to 1968 and the second one to 1995. Before Cavallini, Taurisano, too, had based his own edition (the original one of 1928 and the revised one of 1947) on the Casanatense. Earlier editions, instead, from Gigli's to Fiorilli's, had followed codex T.II.9 of the Communal Library in Siena.

37. *Dialogo*, pp. xlv–xlvi.

38. Ibid., p. xii.

The first printed editions, starting with the oldest one by Baldassare Azzoguidi in Bologna around 1472, followed the chapter division.[39] The division of the *Dialogue* into four treatises (subdivided, in their turn, into 167 chapters) appeared for the first time in the 1579 edition by Onofrio Farri in Venice. This structure was faithfully preserved in all later editions for nearly four centuries.[40]

The edition by Onofrio Farri has the following heading: *Dialogo della serafica vergine e sposa di Christo S. Catherina da Siena / Diviso in quattro trattati / Nel quale profondissimamente si tratta della Provvidenza di Dio / Et un breve compendio della sua vita; ecc.* ("Dialogue of the seraphic virgin and bride of Christ St. Catherine of Siena / Divided into four treatises / Discussing the providence of God in great depth / And a short compendium of her life; etc."). The Venetian publisher isolated the words relative to the treatises from the chapter rubrics and printed them in bold letters framed with embellishments. In this manner, the Italian word *trattato* took on the meaning of "treatise" or "treatment" (*trattamento*), which was completely different from its original meaning in the rubric, where it was meant to indicate simply what was said about a certain topic. By stretching the meaning of the term *trattato* found in the rubrics of chapters 9, 65, 135, and 154, Farri created a partition that, at least in the first two treatises, has no relation to the text and makes it more difficult to understand.[41]

This incoherent division was preserved by all those who published later editions of the *Dialogue* for nearly four centuries. Some scholars even maintained that the term *trattato* constitutes almost

---

39. A number of the first editions, after the one by Azzoguidi, were printed in Venice, such as the ones by Mathio di Codeca (1494), Lazaro di Soardi (1504), Cesare Arrivabeno (1517), and Piero de' Nicolini (1547). On the early Italian editions, see M.-H. Laurent, "Essai de bibliographie catherinienne. Les premières éditions italiennes (1474[–75]–1500)," in *Archivum Fratrum Praedicatorum* 20 (1950), pp. 348–68.

40. Since Azzoguidi's edition in 1472, the *Dialogue* has been the subject of more than seventy editions, including the various translations into Latin, French, English, Spanish, German, and other languages.

41. *Dialogo*, pp. xiii–xiv.

a sort of original division because it was used by Catherine herself.[42] Others have made an effort to match the four treatises with the four petitions of the *Dialogue*, without attaining plausible results.

As was noted earlier, credit is due to Giuliana Cavallini for having brought back to light the original structure of the *Dialogue*. She found—at first inadvertently—that there were three elements in each chapter of the work that regularly followed one another: petition, response, and thanksgiving. After a more careful analysis, Cavallini observed that these three essential elements were linked to others that confirmed the theory of their structural function in the architecture of the *Dialogue*: the presentation of a certain topic almost always ended with a recapitulation of the subject matter, and the thanksgiving grew into a song of praise attuned to the same topic. Confirmation of the validity of this pattern, which Cavallini had identified solely on the basis of internal criteria, came from a comparison with the Casanatense codex. In making the comparison, in fact, Cavallini observed that the initial capital letters in the Casanatense corresponded to the divisions of the new structure she had discovered.[43]

Cavallini's edition is therefore articulated into eight logically connected parts, preceded by an introduction and followed by a conclusion containing the recapitulation of all its parts and a final thanksgiving.[44] With the recovery of its original structure, the *Dialogue* reveals its unified structure and allows for a "proper appreciation of its value."[45]

---

42. See R. Fawtier, *Sainte Catherine de Sienne—Essai de critique des sources*, vol. 2, op. cit., p. 350; and Santa Caterina da Siena, *Dialogo della Divina Provvidenza* (I. Taurisano, ed.), op. cit., p. xxii.

43. *Dialogo*, pp. xvi–xvii.

44. In Cavallini's edition, the *Dialogue* is articulated as follows: Prologue (chs. 1–2); Way of Perfection (chs. 3–13); Dialogue (chs. 14–25); Doctrine of the Bridge (chs. 26–87); Doctrine of the Tears (chs. 88–97); Doctrine of the Truth (chs. 98–108); Mystical Body of the Holy Church (chs. 109–134); Divine Providence (chs. 135–153); Obedience (chs. 154–165); Conclusion (chs. 166–167).

45. Ibid., p. xvi.

6. *DIALOGUE'S* AUTHENTICITY

Tradition unanimously attributes the book to Catherine. As indicated earlier, this is attested by Raymond of Capua in his *Legenda maior*, by Guidini in his Memorial, and by various depositions at the Castellano Process. However, some scholars have asked whether her disciples might not have added minor interpolations to the text. For example, Motzo maintains that Catherine entrusted the book and all other writings to her disciples in letter 373, otherwise known as her spiritual will, asking them to conduct a revision of them. This scholar heavily insists that this revision occurred, basing his claim primarily on the Casanatense codex, which was the subject of his research and in which he perceived a certain stringent theological language regarding the Eucharist that was not present in codex T.II.9 at the Communal Library in Siena or codex T.6.5 at the Estense Library in Modena. From this, Motzo infers that the revisers made some changes (though minor ones), which do not affect his conclusion that Catherine's work has come to us just as she dictated it.[46]

Taurisano, on the other hand, rejects the term *revisers*, bringing attention to the respect that Catherine's disciples had for her dictation, which they considered to be of supernatural origin.[47] According to this scholar, Raymond of Capua provides a clear example of this attitude in the Prologue of his *Legenda maior*, where he writes:

If we turn next to the *Book* which she composed in her own vernacular, manifestly at the dictation of the Holy Spirit, who could

---

46. B. R. Motzo, "Per un'edizione critica delle opere di S. Caterina da Siena," op. cit., pp. 111–41.

47. On this point, G. D'Urso writes that Catherine's contemporaries had such admiration for her and the charismatic origin of her words that "they would never have dared dispute the authenticity of her writings and of the autographs of which they so eagerly sought to get copies" ("Il dialogo di S. Caterina: un'intervista col re del cielo," in L. Trenti and B. Klange Addabbo (eds.), *Con l'occhio e col lume—Atti del corso seminariale di studi su S. Caterina da Siena (25 settembre—7 ottobre 1995)*, Siena 1999, pp. 39–51, at p. 51).

imagine or believe that it was the work of a woman? Its style is so sublime that it is quite a task to make a corresponding Latin version equal to it in sublimity. This has been my own experience in making the Latin translation of it which I am engaged on at present.[48]

Taurisano ultimately affirms that it would be better to use the term *proofreaders* (*correttori*) rather than *revisers* (*revisori*).[49]

7. CONCLUSION

In his research regarding the composition of the *Dialogue*, Dupré Theseider points out that this work "has an undeniably unified character that also presumes a single author."[50] Similarly, Cavallini talks about a "characteristic imprint" marking Catherine's style, such that "Catherine can speak about truths as ancient as the world itself and use images already used by others, but the linguistic style remains unmistakably her own."[51] In conclusion, scholars agree that the *Dialogue*, in its entirety, is the authentic work of Catherine.[52]

48. *Life*, p. 7, para. 8.
49. Santa Caterina da Siena, *Dialogo della Divina Provvidenza* (I. Taurisano, ed.), op. cit., p. xx.
50. E. Dupré Theseider, "Sulla composizione del *Dialogo*," op. cit., p. 199.
51. *Dialogo*, p. xxxix.
52. Dominique de Courcelles has observed that, even assuming that the Dominicans have somewhat revised the *Dialogue* by inserting in it some passages from her letters, the fact remains that this book is the result of Catherine's personal work, which retains her typical rhythm and sonority (D. de Courcelles, "Le Dialogue de Catherine de Sienne ou l'accès du sujet intelligent créé à la perfection ultime: du langage thomiste au langage de l'âme," in *Archives d'Histoire Littéraire et Doctrinale du Moyen Age* 62 (1995), pp. 71–135, at p. 83).

Chapter 4

Composition and Authenticity of the *Prayers*

The title *Prayers* is applied to a collection of prayers attributed to Catherine, the majority of which are considered to date back to her final years, especially her stay in Rome. Unlike the *Letters* and the *Dialogue*, the *Prayers* were not dictated but rather written by her disciples, perhaps even without her knowledge, while she was fully absorbed in prayer.[1] The rubric placed at the beginning of the codices at the time they were collected makes it clear that whatever is available today is just a small portion of the whole body of Catherine's prayers.

There are two primary collections of the *Prayers*, a Latin set and an Italian set, in addition to several other codices.[2] In 1500, Aldo Manuzio published a set of twenty-six prayers at end of his edition of Catherine's *Letters*.[3] In a certain sense, that publication came to

---

1. On this, see Bartolomeo Dominici's deposition at the Castellano Process (M.-H. Laurent (ed.), "Il Processo Castellano," op. cit., pp. 328–29).

2. The more complete collections of *Prayers* are the two in Latin in T.II.7 (S1) at the Communal Library in Siena and XIV,24 (R) of the Archive of the Dominicans' General Curia at Saint Sabina in Rome. These two collections comprise twenty-two prayers in the same order. Codex T.II.7 contains also the collection, in the vernacular, of seventeen prayers in a different order from the Latin series. Some prayers in the vernacular can also be found in I.VI.14 of the Communal Library in Siena and Codex (Mo).

3. Aldo Manuzio published in Venice, in September 1500, 353 letters by Catherine, together with the Italian version of 26 prayers. The Aldo Manuzio in question is known as Aldo the Elder (1449–1515), a well-known publisher and humanist and an innovator in the typographical trade.

constitute the canon of the *Prayers*, which was later handed down from edition to edition. In 1707, Gigli published the same twenty-six prayers, with only minor corrections, in the fourth volume of his edition of Catherine's writings.

Some scholars have excluded the twenty-fifth prayer from the collection. This is the famous invocation of the Holy Spirit that, according to Caffarini's testimony, was supposedly written by Catherine herself.[4] Fawtier, who conducted quite a thorough investigation of the *Prayers*, particularly the dates when they were written, does not accept the authenticity of the twenty-fifth prayer because, in his opinion, "none of the manuscripts that have preserved the text of the prayers contains it."[5] Yet, this affirmation does not seem to take into account Sienese manuscript I.VI.14, with which Fawtier is familiar and which he even cites in other contexts.[6]

Grion, too, rejects the prayer in question as belonging to the set of Catherine's prayers, primarily on the basis of "very serious internal problems," though knowing that it is contained in the Vienna Codex (Mo) discovered by Dupré Theseider. According to Grion, this is, in fact, the only trinitarian prayer in which Catherine—contrary to her usual manner—does not attribute power to the Father, wisdom to the Son, and mercy to the Holy Spirit. From this, Grion concludes that, among the *Prayers*, there is no "prayer so imprecise in its terminology and in the attributes given to the Persons of the Trinity" as the twenty-fifth prayer, thus affecting its authenticity.[7]

Cavallini, who authored the first critical edition of the *Prayers*,[8] instead preserved the canon of twenty-six prayers. The reason for

---

4. M.-H. Laurent (ed.), "Il Processo Castellano," op. cit., pp. 62–63.

5. R. Fawtier, *Sainte Catherine de Sienne—Essai de critique des sources*, vol. 2, op. cit., p. 354.

6. Ibid., pp. 354 and 359.

7. A. Grion, *Santa Caterina da Siena*, op. cit., p. 177.

8. S. Caterina da Siena, *Le Orazioni* (G. Cavallini,ed.), Roma, 1978. This was the first critical edition of Catherine's prayers, prepared on the basis of all the available manuscripts. This edition carries the Italian and Latin versions side by side to facilitate the understanding of the text. The Latin translation was the work of Catherine's disciples, who were familiar with her thought and language.

not excluding the twenty-fifth prayer is its presence in two reliable codices, in addition to the circumstances under which it was supposedly composed, namely Catherine's unique psychological state at the time. (Evidence of that psychological state can be found in letter 272, addressed to Raymond of Capua, as well as in other letters from the same time period.)

With the exception of the twenty-fifth prayer, scholars accept the authenticity of the *Prayers*, which have been endowed with a significant status—and not merely a secondary one—among Catherine's writings. It is therefore lamentable, as Fawtier rightly notes, that only a small number of Catherine's prayers have survived.[9]

* * *

The conclusion of this first part is that the great majority of scholars are in agreement on the authenticity of Catherine's writings. It is also true, though, that the text of these writings is available through manuscript collections more or less directly attributable to several of her disciples. Hence one has to accept the fact that, between Catherine's text and the reader, there is invariably the interposition of the different personalities of the amanuenses (which is why some scholars prefer the word *dictations* to *writings*). In any event, this fact and the consequent likelihood of minor interpolations do not invalidate the substantial authenticity, and the undeniably internal consistency, of Catherine's writings.

9. R. Fawtier, *Sainte Catherine de Sienne—Essai de critique des sources*, vol. 2, op. cit., p. 360.

PART II

ANALYSIS

Textual Examination: The Meaning and Role of Discretion in Catherine's Writings

In this second part, Catherine's writings are analyzed to determine the mean-
ing of discretion and the role that discretion, and prudence (which, as is
shown, is its synonym), play in Catherine's reflection.[1] *This part comprises*

1. To provide immediately an inventory of passages, the term *discretion* occurs
twenty-five times in the *Dialogue* in these chapters: 9 (8 times), 10 (2), 11 (9), 14 (1),
46 (2), 99 (1), 119 (1), and 163 (1). It occurs thirty-six times in these *Letters*: 33 (1),
42 (1), 58 (1), 173 (2), 199 (1), 213 (22), 215 (1), 245 (1), 265 (1), 305 (1), 307 (2), 330
(1), and 341 (1). It occurs only twice in these *Prayers*: 9 (1) and 11 (1). The adjective
discreet, referred to the soul, can be found only once, in letter 154. The adverb *discreetly*
occurs five times in the *Dialogue*: 9 (3 times), 11 (1), and 131 (1). It occurs six times in
the *Letters*: 213 (5 times) and 173 (1). The term *prudence* occurs twenty-one times in
the *Dialogue*, in these chapters: 7 (1), 11 (2), 63 (1), 66 (1), 70 (1), 71 (2), 106 (4), 135
(3), 140 (1), 144 (1), 147 (1), 151 (2), and 159 (1). It occurs thirty-three times in these
Letters: 11 (1), 26 (1), 84 (1), 102 (1), 154 (1), 189 (1), 242 (1), 250 (1), 266 (5), 267 (1),
279 (1), 318 (1), 330 (1), 340 (1), 341 (1), 343 (1), 349 (3), 350 (1), 351 (1), 353 (1), 358
(1), 370 (5), and 373 (1). It occurs five times in these *Prayers*: 8 (3) and 11 (2). The adjective *prudent* occurs only twice in the *Dialogue*: 142 (1) and 145 (1). It occurs thirteen
times in these *Letters*: 26 (1), 71 (1), 122 (1), 245 (1), 250 (1), 266 (2), 272 (1), 335 (1),
340 (1), 353 (1), 372 (1), and 382 (1). It occurs twice in the *Prayers*: 10 (1) and 11 (1).
The adverb *prudently* appears four times in these *Letters*: 154 (1), 266 (1), 330 (1), and
341 (1).

three chapters. The first one (chapter 5) examines the Dialogue, which is the work of Catherine's spiritual maturity and therefore an appropriate starting point in this investigation.[2] Chapters 6 and 7 then address, respectively, the Letters and the Prayers.

2. According to S. Noffke, the *Dialogue* "serves as the touchstone for the study of thematic developments in her other works" ("Demythologizing Catherine: The Wealth of Internal Evidence," in *Spirituality Today* 32 (1980), pp. 4–12, at p. 8).

Chapter 5

A First Approach

Discretion in the Dialogue

1. INTRODUCTION

In the *Dialogue*, there are three chapters (9–11) specifically dedicated to discretion. However, these chapters do not certainly exhaust Catherine's reflection on the topic. There are passages outside of these chapters in which the term *discretion* (*discrezione*) is used, and there are also passages referring to *prudence* (*prudenzia*) and to other notions closely linked to discretion. Hence there is a composite picture that needs to be examined in some detail to arrive at some preliminary finding on the meaning and role of discretion in Catherine's spiritual journey.

2. DISCRETION IN CHAPTERS 9 TO 11

Catherine introduces the notion of discretion at the beginning of chapter 9. Referring to penance, she writes that penance without discretion is a hindrance to perfection, because without "the discerning light of the knowledge" of oneself and of God's goodness, penance "would be undiscerning," not loving what God most loves and not hating what God most hates.[1] In the same chapter, Catherine provides a definition of *discretion*, which is

> the true knowledge a soul ought to have of herself and of me [i.e. God], and through this knowledge she finds her roots. It is joined to charity like an engrafted shoot. Charity, it is true, has many offshoots, like a tree with many branches. But what gives life to both the tree and its branches is its root, so long as that root is planted in the soil of humility. For humility is the governess and wet nurse of the charity into which this branch of [discretion] is engrafted. Now the source of humility, as I have already told you, is the soul's true knowledge of herself and of my goodness. So only when [discretion] is rooted in humility is it virtuous, producing life-giving fruit and willingly yielding what is due to everyone.[2]

From this it is already evident how difficult it is to interpret Catherine's language, filled as it is with repetitions and occasional imprecisions, and reflecting a constant effort to synthesize.[3] Her linguistic style stiffens the challenge of comprehension, especially because Catherine uses images in a very personal manner. Upon close examination, these difficulties with interpretation are primarily due to the fact that Catherine's language is the expression of her mystical experience. If one accepts the idea that mystical experience can transcend intellectual reflection, it is likewise necessary to accept that the language expressing such experience may present imprecisions and may sometimes be difficult to understand.

The foregoing is a perfect example of what has just been noted. Discretion is first identified with knowledge of oneself and God, but

---

1. *Dialogue*, p. 40, ch. 9 (*Dialogo*, pp. 26–27).
2. *Dialogue*, p. 40, ch. 9 (*Dialogo*, pp. 27–28).
3. T. S. Centi, "Luci e ombre sul tomismo di S. Caterina da Siena," in *Atti del Congresso Internazionale di Studi Cateriniani, Siena-Roma 24–29 aprile 1980*, op. cit., pp. 76–92, at p. 83.

then, in the very next statement, it seems to derive from, and have its roots in, this knowledge. Last, discretion is described as a branch engrafted in the tree of charity planted in the soil of humility.

In summary, there is no precise image of discretion. However, it is possible to identify several essential elements: the tree of charity and the tree of discretion, by its side, are planted in humility, which seems to derive from the knowledge of oneself and God. This already shows how discretion is strictly tied to charity, humility, and knowledge of oneself and God.

There are other passages in which charity, humility, and knowledge of oneself and God are tied to discretion. For example, in chapter 10, Catherine explains the relationship between charity and humility by resorting to the image of the circle traced on the ground, having at its center "a tree sprouting with a shoot grafted into its side. The tree finds its nourishment in the soil within the expanse of the circle, but uprooted from the soil it would die fruitless."[4] The meaning of this image of the circle can better be understood in light of what she writes later:

> The circle in which this tree's root, the soul's love, must grow is true knowledge of herself, knowledge that is joined to me [i.e. God], who like the circle have neither beginning nor end. You can go round and round within this circle, finding neither end nor beginning, yet never leaving the circle. This knowledge of yourself, and of me within yourself, is grounded in the soil of true humility, which is as great as the expanse of the circle (which is the knowledge of yourself united with me, as I have said). But if your knowledge of yourself were isolated from me there would be no full circle at all. Instead, there would be a beginning in self-knowledge, but apart from me it would end in confusion.[5]

---

4. *Dialogue*, p. 41, ch. 10 (*Dialogo*, p. 29).
5. *Dialogue*, pp. 41–42, ch. 10 (*Dialogo*, p. 30).

The circle therefore represents the knowledge one has of himself. This knowledge, being united with God who has no beginning or end, becomes also knowledge of God. How is this knowledge of oneself, which is authentic knowledge because it leads to knowledge of God, attained? Catherine's response is that the soul attains it when it recognizes that all it has comes from God, considering itself worthy of punishment for its ingratitude and negligence in the use of the time and graces received: the soul repays itself with contempt and regret for sin, and this is precisely the work of the virtue of discretion, "rooted in self-knowledge and true humility."[6]

It is by the action of divine grace that the soul discovers that it has received its being and every other good thing from God. This knowledge, which the soul acquires of itself and its nothingness, prompts it to hate its sins. In chapter 9, while discussing the will, Catherine introduces another image of discretion, which is now "the knife that kills and cuts off all selfish love to its foundation in self-will."[7] This selfish love is the origin of all sins: it is loving oneself for the sake of oneself and not loving oneself for the sake of God.[8] Once man's will is subordinated to God's will, the soul desires to pay its "debt" to God, and it is the task of discretion to indicate the path to be taken to pay this debt. In this way, by its directing role, discretion appears as the "light" that "dissolves all darkness, dissipates ignorance, and seasons every virtue and virtuous deed." Again, it is discretion that "has a prudence that cannot be deceived, a strength that is invincible, a constancy right up to the end, reaching as it does from heaven to

6. *Dialogue*, pp. 40–41, ch. 9 (*Dialogo*, p. 28).
7. *Dialogue*, p. 43, ch. 11 (*Dialogo*, p. 33).
8. G. M. Cavalcoli rightly points out that love of self is an Augustinian expression to indicate the capital sin of pride, a sin that Catherine in fact derives from the love of self. (In other passages from Catherine, the derivation is the other way round, but what counts is the inseparable connection between pride and love of self.) Whoever sins of this love of self wants to replace God as the foundation of moral law, creating himself the principles of his own conduct ("La vittoria sull 'amor proprio' nella dottrina di S. Caterina da Siena (Parte prima)," in *Divinitas* 44 (2001), pp. 3–16 (part 1), at pp. 10–15, and pp. 115–40 (part 2), at p. 115).

earth," namely from the knowledge of God to the knowledge of one-self, from the love of God to the love of neighbor: discretion's "truly humble prudence evades every devilish and creaturely snare, and with unarmed hand—that is, through suffering—it overcomes the devil and the flesh."[9] Therefore, discretion seems to order not only such moral virtues as prudence, fortitude, and perseverance but also charity, which is "showered by the light of true discretion" in such a way that discretion sets no limit to the love of the soul for God, but still sets the conditions of the love for neighbor. Hence a soul desiring grace loves God "without limit or condition," and loves neighbor with "measured and ordered charity."[10]

In conclusion, chapters 9 through 11 of the *Dialogue* already reveal that discretion is one of the fundamental notions in Catherine's spirituality. This preliminary conclusion is confirmed by the examination of those passages, outside of chapters 9 through 11, where the term *discretion* and its opposite, *indiscretion*, can be found.

3. THE TERM *DISCRETION* OUTSIDE OF CHAPTERS 9 TO 11

There are not many passages in the *Dialogue*, outside of chapters 9 to 11, that contain the word *discretion*. The expression "time of discretion" occurs in chapter 14 and refers to the time of maturity in which the soul, while having received God's grace through baptism, may still be disposed to either good or evil;[11] a similar expression occurs in chapter 46, where Catherine writes of those who reach the "age of discretion" having exercised themselves in virtue and keeping the light of faith received through baptism.[12]

---

9. *Dialogue*, pp. 44–45, ch. 11 (*Dialogo*, p. 36).
10. *Dialogue*, p. 44, ch. 11 (*Dialogo*, pp. 34–5).
11. *Dialogue*, p. 53, ch. 14 (*Dialogo*, p. 50).
12. *Dialogue*, p. 94, ch. 46 (*Dialogo*, p. 119).

Then, in chapter 99, Catherine writes that the "perfect," namely those who have distanced themselves from the ordinary ways of the world and have embraced harsh and extraordinary penance, are guided by the "light of discretion," which allows them to be humble and truly know themselves and God.[13] This "light of discretion" is the same light that shines through such "glorious ministers" of the Church as Augustine and Thomas Aquinas, who by their holy and honest lives and the light of their knowledge have enlightened the souls of those who were living in the darkness of mortal sin: the "pearl of justice" shone in them "with true humility and blazing charity, with enlightened [discretion]."[14]

The final part of the *Dialogue*, which is entirely dedicated to the praise of obedience, contains another passage in which *discretion* plays a decisive role. It is when Catherine writes that obedience is crowned with perseverance so that, even when the superiors, for "lack of discretion," impose great burdens on obedience, this does not make obedience falter.[15] While the "light of discretion" is always associated with the "perfect," lack of discretion (or "darkness of indiscretion") is attributed to sinners. For example, in chapter 122, one reads that injustice proceeds from selfishness and the "dark lack of discretion."[16] Likewise, the image of the "tree of charity," accompanied by the bud of discretion (see chapters 9 to 10), comes back in a negative light with regard to wicked men lacking discretion:

I made them trees of love through the life of grace, which they received in holy baptism. But they have become trees of death, because they are dead. Do you know where this tree of death is

---

13. *Dialogue*, p. 186, ch. 99 (*Dialogo*, p. 274).

14. *Dialogue*, p. 223, ch. 119 (*Dialogo*, p. 336). See also what Catherine writes of the "faithful and virile" shepherds in ch. 131 (*Dialogue*, p. 265; *Dialogo*, p. 409).

15. *Dialogue*, p. 353, ch. 163 (*Dialogo*, p. 568). In the subsequent chapter, Catherine adds that, with the "indiscreet burdens" of heavy commands, "the virtue of obedience is gained along with patience, her sister" (*Dialogue*, p. 355, ch. 164; *Dialogo*, pp. 570–71).

16. *Dialogue*, p. 234, ch. 122 (*Dialogo*, pp. 354–55).

rooted? In the height of pride, which is nourished by their sensual selfishness. Its core is impatience and its offshoot is the lack of any [discretion].[17]

Sinners who fall into false judgments are indiscreet: their selfishness, indecency, pride, avarice, envy are grounded in their "perverse lack of [discretion]."[18]

4. PRUDENCE IN THE *DIALOGUE* AND ITS RELATION TO DISCRETION

Catherine also uses the term *prudence* (*prudenzia*). In several passages, prudence is linked to such other virtues as temperance and patience.[19] At other times, prudence and light are mentioned side by side in reference to the inner harmony of the soul.[20] More specifically, prudence is linked to the "light of the intellect" and to knowledge:

A soul who walks with scant prudence and not step by step finds little. But one who has much finds much. For the more the soul tries to free her affection and bind it to me by the light of understanding, the more she will come to know. One who knows more loves more, and loving more, enjoys more.[21]

17. *Dialogue*, p. 73, ch. 31 (*Dialogo*, pp. 85–86). See also *Dialogue*, p. 231, ch. 121 (*Dialogo*, pp. 350–51).

18. *Dialogue*, p. 76, ch. 35 (*Dialogo*, p. 91).

19. See the passage on virtues in *Dialogue*, p. 37, ch. 7 (*Dialogo*, p. 23). See also *Dialogue*, pp. 44–45, ch. 11 (*Dialogo*, p. 36); *Dialogue*, p. 113, ch. 59 (*Dialogo*, p. 151); *Dialogue*, p. 119, ch. 63 (*Dialogo*, p. 162); *Dialogue*, p. 305, ch. 145 (*Dialogo*, pp. 479–80); *Dialogue*, p. 321, ch. 151 (*Dialogo*, p. 511); *Dialogue*, pp. 342–43, ch. 159 (*Dialogo*, p. 548).

20. See the passage on light and prudence in *Dialogue*, p. 310, ch. 147 (*Dialogo*, pp. 489–90). See also *Dialogue*, p. 132, ch. 70 (*Dialogo*, p. 184); *Dialogue*, p. 289, ch. 140 (*Dialogo*, p. 451); *Dialogue*, p. 302, ch. 144 (*Dialogo*, p. 475).

21. *Dialogue*, p. 126, ch. 66 (*Dialogo*, p. 174). See also *Dialogue*, pp. 199–200, ch. 106 (*Dialogo*, pp. 295–96).

It is "gentle prudence" that allows the soul to discern whether a vision comes from God or from the devil: a soul that "chooses to behave humbly and prudently" cannot be deluded.[22] Prudence is also linked to the sacraments and the "great hunger for communion," which certain souls experience when God tests them by making them "cautious and prudent" so that they may not imprudently relax their hunger.[23] Finally, in chapter 135, prudence and providence are mentioned in reference to the Father:

> So, to take away this death, dearest daughter, I gave humankind the Word, my only-begotten Son, thus providing for your need with great prudence and providence. I say "with prudence" because with the bait of your humanity and the hook of my divinity I caught the devil, who could not recognize my Truth. This Truth, the incarnate Word, came to destroy and put an end to his lie, which he had used to deceive humankind.[24]

These selected passages show how prudence is often linked to such other virtues as humility, patience, and perseverance; how it is paired with light (and specifically the light of knowledge); and what an important role it plays in the discernment of visions, in "knowing with prudence" the deceptions and false visions or consolations from the devil.

All of this leads to suggest that the meaning of prudence draws close to the meaning of discretion, with the exception of the last citation, in which prudence is paired with providence in reference to

22. *Dialogue*, pp. 133–34, ch. 71 (*Dialogo*, pp. 185–86). See also *Dialogue*, p. 200, ch. 106 (*Dialogo*, p. 298).

23. *Dialogue*, p. 294, ch. 142 (*Dialogo*, p. 460).

24. *Dialogue*, p. 278, ch. 135 (*Dialogo*, p. 431). At note 5 of the Italian edition, on the same page, G. Cavallini writes that "the deceiver is deceived by his own ignorance of the incarnated Truth. There is here a singular parallel with a passage in Maxim the Confessor (*Cent.* 1,10)."

God. In other words, apart from this exception, in the *Dialogue* the terms *prudence* and *discretion* are essentially synonymous.

5. DISCRETION AND AUTHENTIC KNOWLEDGE

In addition to the passages in the *Dialogue* where the term *discretion* appears with its synonym, *prudence*, the notion of discretion is occasionally reflected in other concepts such as "authentic knowledge," which is knowledge of oneself and God.

This authentic knowledge, also identified with discretion in chapter 9, is such an essential element in Catherine's reflection that her spirituality has been defined as the doctrine of twofold knowledge: knowledge of God—the absolute Being, the first sweet Truth and infinite Love—together with knowledge of oneself, one's nothingness and one's sin and disordered self-love. If one can speak of a spiritual itinerary in Catherine, authentic knowledge is its starting point. At the beginning of the *Dialogue*, one reads:

> A soul rises up, restless with tremendous desire for God's honor and the salvation of souls. She has for some time exercised herself in virtue and has become accustomed to dwelling in the cell of self-knowledge in order to know better God's goodness toward her, since upon knowledge follows love. And loving, she seeks to pursue truth and clothe herself in it.[25]

This "cell of self-knowledge" allows everyone to appreciate his or her nothingness on the ontological level and the moral depravity of sin; it is through this knowledge that a soul learns how man is nothing while God is everything. It is by divine grace that the soul reaches authentic knowledge through that light of faith that is the "mirror of

---

25. *Dialogue*, p. 25, ch. 1 (*Dialogo*, p. 1).

God," where the soul sees both its own dignity and its own unworthi-ness.[26] The soul, "knowing itself in its non-being," finds true humility in this knowledge, which is to say an awareness of its own nothing-ness, which is one of the main themes of Catherine's spirituality. In fact, the tree of charity and the shoot of discretion by its side have their roots in humility.[27] Knowledge of oneself and God, together with humility and charity, are inextricably linked: it is through the knowledge of self that one attains the truth, but knowledge of self alone is insufficient, as it must be "seasoned by and joined with"[28] knowing God. This is how the soul finds, at one time, humility and contempt for self, as well as the fire of God's charity, arriving at love for neighbor.

Having thus identified the key passages on discretion, this study may now proceed with investigating which role discretion plays in Catherine's spiritual itinerary, examining its constitutive elements with a view to sketching a first outline of the concept.

6. THE ROLE OF DISCRETION IN CATHERINE'S SPIRITUAL ITINERARY

Which are the fundamental steps of the spiritual journey through which a soul attains perfection or the "excellence of unitive love" in God?[29]

The first step, and the basis of all inner life, is authentic knowl-edge, which is knowledge of man's depravity and God's infinite goodness. It is by way of this authentic knowledge that one discov-ers the chasm between the littleness of man and the infinitude of

---

26. *Dialogue*, p. 48, ch. 13 (*Dialogo*, p. 41). See also *Dialogue*, pp. 365–66, ch. 167 (*Dialogo*, p. 586).

27. *Dialogue*, p. 41, ch. 9 (*Dialogo*, p. 29).

28. *Dialogue*, p. 158, ch. 86 (*Dialogo*, pp. 226–27). See also *Dialogue*, p. 118, ch. 63 (*Dialogo*, p. 160).

29. *Dialogue*, p. 362, ch. 166 (*Dialogo*, p. 580).

God. Thanks to this knowledge, one learns that God is "He who is" while man is "nothing" in himself, since his being is participation in (namely exists only by virtue of) divine being.[30]

This authentic knowledge is transcendent knowledge because it goes beyond what can be known in natural terms, to the point that this knowledge must come from God to be authentic. It is only by knowing himself in God, and the relationship that exists between himself and God, that man is able to attain true knowledge of himself. In Catherine's spirituality, these two forms of knowledge—the reason for talking about a twofold knowledge—are actually one, given their inseparability. In fact, knowledge of self without knowledge of God would lead man to confusion and despair; knowledge of God without knowledge of self would lead him to presumptuousness. Authentic knowledge is acquired by the light of the intellect illuminated by faith. But the natural intellect alone is not up to this high task. For this reason, authentic knowledge must necessarily be supernatural knowledge: it is a gift of divine grace.

What then is this supernatural light that illuminates the intellect and through which the soul comes to know itself in God? For Catherine, faith is a "pupil" at the center of the eye of the intellect that raises it up to the knowledge of the intimate life of God. This pupil is placed in the eye of the natural intellect at baptism: it is a light that shows man the road to follow to attain eternal life. The intellect has its own light, just as faith does; the latter serves itself of the natural light of the intellect, which then leads man "in the way of truth" once it has been illuminated by the supernatural light of faith. The following passage from chapter 98 is explicit on this subject:

> In baptism, through the power of my only-begotten Son's blood, you received the form of faith. If you exercise this faith by virtue with the light of reason, reason will in turn be enlightened by

30. "You will find humility in the knowledge of yourself when you see that even your own existence comes not from yourself but from me, for I loved you before you came into being" (*Dialogue*, p. 29, ch. 4; *Dialogo*, p. 10).

faith, and such faith will give you light and lead you in the way of truth. With this light you will reach me, the true Light; without it you would come to darkness.[31]

As Garrigou-Lagrange rightly points out, Catherine's thought presents faith "not only as required obedience to a revealed formula proposed by the Church, but as intense and radiant life."[32] According to Catherine, man can only attain knowledge of himself and of God through faith, through this authentic knowledge that allows man to know himself in God and leads him to stoop down into "the valley of humility."[33]

The humility that shows man his exact value in the sight of God derives from knowing human nothingness and the moral depravity of sin, on the one hand, and divine "everything" and God's infinite love, on the other. Humility is ultimately the fruit of this authentic knowledge because it comes from recognizing that human beings are nothing in themselves, inasmuch as they receive everything from God. Yet knowing oneself in God also means knowing God's love and mercy, so that, if humility—which is awareness of human nothingness and depravity—is based upon this knowledge, then charity also proceeds from this authentic knowledge. For Catherine, in fact, truly knowing God means loving him, because love follows understanding: "the more they know, the more they love, and the more they love, the more they know."[34]

It is only by understanding how much God loves him that man, in turn, can love God and recognize that he has been given life and offered salvation by divine mercy.[35] Therefore, if knowledge of human depravity leads to humility, knowledge of God's goodness and

31. *Dialogue*, p. 185, ch. 98 (*Dialogo*, p. 271).
32. R. Garrigou-Lagrange, "La foi selon sainte Catherine de Sienna," in *La Vie Spirituelle* 45 (1935), pp. 236–49, at p. 237.
33. *Dialogue*, p. 29, ch. 4 (*Dialogo*, pp. 9–10).
34. *Dialogue*, p. 157, ch. 85 (*Dialogo*, p. 226).
35. *Dialogue*, p. 71, ch. 30 (*Dialogo*, p. 82).

boundless love leads us to love him and everything he loves. In this way, a soul that attains knowledge of itself and of God in the light of faith and therefore attains humility rises in God's love and immediately yields "what is due to everyone."[36] It is here that discretion intervenes.

As was seen earlier, Catherine's image of discretion is a "child" of the tree of charity, planted together with it in the ground of humility, which is in turn circumscribed by the circle of knowledge of self in God. In this image, discretion seems tightly bound with authentic knowledge, humility, and charity. Discretion is therefore presented as a child or a bud of the tree of charity. This sapling is so thoroughly grafted to the tree of charity that "every fruit produced by this tree is seasoned with [discretion], and this unites them all."[37]

If the tree of charity and mother of virtue produces all fruits, which is to say all virtues, then this means that her "child," discretion, participates in the generation of these fruits or virtues. In fact, one might say that this bud of discretion is "the first thing that the saint asks the tree of charity to produce."[38] At this point, it is natural to query why discretion holds such an important place in Catherine's spirituality, participating with charity in the generation of all virtues. In other words, why is discretion so important for salvation? Catherine herself offers an answer in chapters 9 and 10 of the *Dialogue*: discretion "immediately renders to each his debts," in that the soul gives glory and praise to God's name for the graces received and, in acknowledging that everything comes from God, gives to itself what it sees itself to be deserving.[39] In addition to rendering the fruit of grace to the soul, discretion ultimately renders the fruit of service to neighbor.[40]

36. *Dialogue*, p. 40, ch. 9 (*Dialogo*, p. 28).

37. *Dialogue*, p. 42, ch. 10 (*Dialogo*, p. 31).

38. A. Lemonnyer, *Notre vie spirituelle à l'école de Sainte Catherine de Sienne*, op. cit., p. 15.

39. *Dialogue*, p. 40, ch. 9 (*Dialogo*, p. 28).

40. *Dialogue*, p. 42, ch. 10 (*Dialogo*, p. 31).

In summary, an analysis of Catherine's spiritual itinerary leads to identifying the privileged place of discretion. With the light of faith, the soul discovers that it is nothing in itself, given that its being and all the goods given to its being come from God. Knowledge of its nothingness and the depravity of sin, on the one hand, and of the infinitude of God, on the other, leads the soul into the valley of humility and love of God. Once the soul is immersed in this love, it experiences hatred and aversion toward its wrongdoings and yearns to pay its debt to God. Discretion intervenes at this point in its guiding role, indicating how the soul should pay its debt to God, to itself, and to its neighbors. Discretion therefore appears to be a rule of conduct shaped by the convergence of authentic knowledge, or knowledge of self in God, humility, and charity. As a rule of conduct, discretion urges man to pay his debt to God, to himself, and to his neighbor in the most appropriate manner because "even a zeal for good can lead us awry if it is not illuminated by this light [i.e. discretion]."[41]

Ultimately, while discretion is genuine spiritual discernment, which is to say the right appreciation of who man is with respect to God, it is also the practical application of that discernment. In other words, discretion is not limited to its speculative aspect but also becomes a practical norm of conduct. In virtue of this, discretion appears to be something truly new whose essential role is not just to show what man should give but also to compel him to give what he should in the most appropriate manner.[42]

(i) In Relation to God

What order should discretion establish in rendering one's debt to God? In other words, how should one love God in light of discretion?

41. G. Cavallini, "La voce di S. Caterina da Siena," in *L'Arbore della Carità* (1963), pp. 19–23, at p. 19.
42. A. Lemonnyer has rightly pointed out that, in Catherine, the knowledge of self and of God is "the foundation of the spiritual life," while discretion "is its living rule," as the norm of all conduct (*Notre vie spirituelle à l'école de Sainte Catherine de Sienne*, op. cit., p. 17).

In chapter 11 of the *Dialogue*, one reads that, God being supreme eternal Truth, discretion "sets neither law nor limit nor condition to the love" for God.[43]

While discretion should not set any limits on love for God, it should enlighten the soul in such a way that its desire to serve God does not mislead it. For example, the soul would be deceived if, after having received in time of prayer the gift of "mental consolation" or another supernatural gift through which God manifests his charity, it were to limit itself to contentment with this consolation by believing that its perfection consists in taking pleasure in gratification. In so doing, the soul would end up omitting service to neighbor by seeking only the pleasure of this consolation and would ultimately wind up seeking not God but its own pleasure, "trying as it were to impose rules on the Holy Spirit."[44]

In the same way, those who strive to place all their delight in the search for peace and tranquility of spirit, particularly through daily prayer, might be deceiving themselves and wind up ignoring the needs of their neighbor. In this manner, their love for God would actually turn into "their own spiritual self-centeredness."[45]

(ii) In Relation to Self

In relation to oneself, discretion has the task of enlightening the soul in such a way that, after having understood that "being and every other grace granted on top of being" come from God, it feels insufficiently grateful for so many gifts and negligent because it has not made adequate use of the time and graces received. Hence, guided by discretion (the "knife that kills and cuts off all selfish love to its foundation in self-will"),[46] the soul "appears deserving of the punishments" and "expresses hatred and displeasure for its wrongs."

43. *Dialogue*, p. 44, ch. 11 (*Dialogo*, p. 34).
44. *Dialogue*, p. 129, ch. 68 (*Dialogo*, p. 179).
45. *Dialogue*, p. 132, ch. 69 (*Dialogo*, p. 182).
46. *Dialogue*, p. 43, ch. 11 (*Dialogo*, p. 33).

Furthermore, discretion is crucial to the way penance is conducted, because penance without discretion is a hindrance to the
soul's perfection.[47] This is so because "perfection consists not only
in beating down and killing the body but in slaying the perverse selfish will."[48] What matters most, in reality, is that the punishment be
endured with infinite remorse and contrition because "God, who is
infinite, would have infinite love and infinite sorrow."[49] It is only in
the light of discretion that a soul desiring to make amends for its
wrongs can complete a true penance. Without discretion, it could
confuse the means, or penance, with its end, which is true contrition
or infinite sorrow for one's sins.

(iii) In Relation to Neighbor

Discretion also exercises its guiding role in relation to one's neighbor. A soul that loves God desires to help its neighbor, because this
is the means that God has given man "to practice and prove" virtue.
Looking out for God's honor, accompanied by thirst for the salvation
of neighbor, is sure evidence that man has God in his soul by grace.[50]
The soul must guard itself against two dangers in its relationship
with neighbor: on the one hand, allowing itself to be influenced by its
neighbor and dragged into sin; on the other hand, forcing its neighbor to walk only in one way along God's path, thereby judging him.
When a soul allows the devil to feed the root of presumption under
the guise of charity for neighbor, man ends up setting himself as the
ultimate judge of the others, thus usurping God's prerogative.[51] To
the contrary, those who are guided by the sweet light rejoice in the
many paths walked by those obeying God's will and in the "many
dwelling places" that exist in the Father's house.[52]

47. *Dialogue*, p. 40, ch. 9 (*Dialogo*, p. 26).
48. *Dialogue*, p. 196, ch. 104 (*Dialogo*, p. 290).
49. *Dialogue*, p. 28, ch. 3 (*Dialogo*, p. 8).
50. *Dialogue*, pp. 36–37, ch. 7 (*Dialogo*, p. 22).
51. *Dialogue*, p. 193, ch. 102 (*Dialogo*, p. 285).
52. *Dialogue*, pp. 189–90, ch. 100 (*Dialogo*, p. 279).

7. CONCLUSION

In conclusion, discretion emerges from the *Dialogue* as a judicious rule of conduct in the moral and spiritual life: it not only brings man to know what he should render to God, to himself, and to others but also shows him the right way to do so and compels him to accomplish it concretely through virtuous action.

Chapter 6

An Additional Perspective

Discretion in the Letters

1. INTRODUCTION

The first of the *Letters* to be analyzed is letter 213, since it deals extensively with discretion, both directly and indirectly, by way of such closely linked concepts as light, knowledge, and debt. After analyzing letter 213, it will be easier to examine a group of letters and highlight the passages referring not only to discretion proper but also to prudence (its synonym), as well as to light, knowledge, and debt.

2. DISCRETION IN LETTER 213

Tommaseo regards letter 213 as one of the masterpieces of Italian prose.[1] Addressed to the *mantellata* Daniella d'Orvieto,[2] this letter begins by pointing out the need for discretion to achieve salvation:

---

1. "One of the noblest letters, one of the highest works of true eloquence in Italian prose" (*Le lettere di S. Caterina da Siena* (with notes by N. Tommaseo), op. cit., vol. 3, p. 227).
2. On Daniella d'Orvieto, see *Letters*, IV, p. 379.

Why is it so necessary? Because it comes from knowledge of our-selves and of God; this knowledge is the house in which it has its roots. It is actually an offshoot of charity, a light and a knowledge the soul has of herself and of God.[3]

Here, too, as in the *Dialogue*, discretion, "the child born of charity," is related to light and knowledge of self and God. As a "discreet light," it guides all the operations of the soul toward the just end of rendering its debt.[4] Having paid our debt of honor to God and having paid our debt to ourselves by despising vice and loving virtue, by that same light we give our neighbors their due.[5]

The three debts are not mentioned one after the other in this let-ter, which is what instead occurs in the *Dialogue*.[6] It is not acciden-tal that the debt of rendering honor and glory to God is mentioned first and isolated from the other two, which are rendering the debt to self and to one's neighbor. In fact, all the operations of the soul are performed with the "discreet light" only because they are ordered to the end of loving God above all else. Having rendered the most important debt, then, which is loving and honoring God, the soul has to render its debt to itself by hating its own vices and seeking virtue, and to its neighbors by loving them benevolently insofar as they have been created by God. This is the main effect of discretion, from the branches of which "grow an infinite variety of fruits."[7]

The unifying character of discretion in relation to the other vir-tues, which had already been expressed in the *Dialogue*,[8] emerges

---

3. *Letters*, III, p. 295 (*Lettere*, III, pp. 227–28).

4. *Letters*, III, p. 296 (*Lettere*, III, p. 228).

5. *Letters*, III, p. 296 (*Lettere*, III, pp. 228–29).

6. In drawing this contrast with the *Dialogue*, it is helpful to recall that most scholars think that the *Letters*, having been subject to fewer interventions than the *Dialogue*, reflect more accurately Catherine's views.

7. *Letters*, III, p. 296 (*Lettere*, III, p. 229).

8. "And every fruit produced by this tree is seasoned with [discretion], and this unites them all, as I have told you" (*Dialogue*, p. 42, ch. 10; *Dialogo*, p. 31).

once more. There are in fact various ways of "tasting" the fruits of the light of discretion:

> Those who are living in the world and have this light gather the fruit of obedience to God's commandments.... If they have children, they pick the fruit of fear of God and nurture those children in that holy fear. If they are rulers, they pick the fruit of justice, choosing with [discretion] to give every person his or her due.... Those who are subordinates gather the fruit of obedience and respect toward their masters.... Those who are religious or religious superiors pick from the branches the sweet pleasing fruit of observance of their rule.[9]

Although the ways of gathering the fruits of discretion are many, and so are the creatures that gather these fruits and the conditions in which they are found, the rule that "instills this virtue of discretion in the soul" is always the same, namely honoring and glorifying God, hating vice and loving virtue in one's life, and being benevolent to one's neighbor. The opposite is the "rule of indiscretion," which results from pride and from the "perversity of selfish love for oneself."[10] Lack of discretion affects the root of a soul's operation, with the consequence that whatever is done, either for self or for others, is rotten.[11]

Discretion is often accompanied by the notions of measure and rule, in letter 213 as in others: it is discretion that leads man down the beaten path of virtue with measure, and the very rule for both body and soul comes from the virtue of discretion.[12] This introduces another characteristic topic of letter 213, namely penance. It is the "rule of discretion" that must determine a just penance. Therefore, if the body is weak and sick, one "should not only relent in fasting but

---

9. *Letters*, III, p. 297 (*Lettere*, III, pp. 229–30).
10. *Letters*, III, p. 298 (*Lettere*, III, p. 231).
11. *Letters*, III, p. 296 (*Lettere*, III, p. 228).
12. *Letters*, III, p. 299 (*Lettere*, III, p. 231).

also eat meat" even multiple times a day.[13] In other words, penance should be a means of perfection and not an end in itself, which is what it becomes for those who aim "to kill the body but not the will" since they are guided by the "rule of indiscretion."[14] When the souls are instead regulated by the light of discretion, they trust in God, not in themselves and their own works:

> They are strong and persevering, since they have put to death within themselves the selfish will that was making them weak and inconstant. Every time is their time; every place is their place.... They find prayer everywhere, because they always carry with them the place where God dwells by grace and where we ought to pray. I mean the house of our soul.... This prayer is humble, because we have come to know our sinfulness, and that we are not.... What is the source of so much good? Charity's daughter, [discretion].[15]

The unifying character of discretion in relation to the other virtues could not emerge more clearly than from this passage.

3. DISCRETION AND PRUDENCE IN THE *LETTERS* OTHER THAN LETTER 213

In letter 265, too, discretion accompanies the notion of measure, when Catherine calls on doing everything with discretion, starting from that sense of measure in the physical life that allows the body to be a fitting instrument to work for God.[16] Discretion is the way for persevering in virtue and ultimately attaining the crown of beatitude.

---

13. *Letters*, III, p. 300 (*Lettere*, III, p. 233).
14. *Letters*, III, p. 300 (*Lettere*, III, p. 234). Already in chapter 9 of the *Dialogue*, Catherine had addressed the theme of discretion while writing on penance.
15. *Letters*, III, pp. 301–3 (*Lettere*, III, pp. 235–37).
16. *Letters*, IV, p. 86 (*Lettere*, IV, p. 134).

In the community, it is the mark of persons of good conscience (letter 55),[17] of good counselors (letter 317),[18] and of wise men (letter 349).[19]

In some letters, Catherine speaks of the "time of discretion," which is the time for reasonable people to strive to maintain the vestment of the grace they received at baptism to attain salvation.[20] It is during the "time of discretion" that every creature endowed with reason, whatever its condition, is called to live the promise made at baptism, renouncing the world and its delights, the devil and its own appetites. For religious women, Catherine notes in letter 58 that, when the "time of discretion" arrives, the brides consecrated to Christ should not be burdened by the baggage of their earthly family, but take possession of the treasure of the Eternal Bridegroom.[21] The "time of discretion" is therefore the time during which, after receiving the light of faith in baptism, man has to exercise virtue. Otherwise, as letter 199 indicates, we will be unable to see, blinded as we are by selfishness and worldly pleasure.[22] Hence (letter 154), it is only once the soul has become "discreet," through the light, that it is able to defend itself against its primary enemies: the world and its vanities and delights, the appetite of the senses that desires inordinately, and the devil with his deceptions and many misleading thoughts and temptations.[23]

In other letters, the reference is not to discretion, but to prudence as its synonym. For example, in letter 266, Catherine assigns prudence an essential role in the spiritual life, affirming that man should consider with prudence how short life is and seek the kingdom of heaven above all else. It is again with prudence that charity's

17. *Letters*, II, p. 470 (*Lettere*, I, p. 214).

18. *Letters*, IV, p. 10 (*Lettere*, V, p. 48).

19. *Letters*, IV, p. 160 (*Lettere*, V, p. 180).

20. See, for example, letter 215: "But if we live to the age of [discretion] we can hold on the invitation given us in holy baptism" (*Letters*, III, p. 7; *Lettere*, III, p. 243).

21. *Letters*, IV, p. 203 (*Lettere*, I, p. 220).

22. *Letters*, III, p. 101 (*Lettere*, III, p. 174).

23. *Letters*, IV, p. 49 (*Lettere*, III, p. 6). See also letter 76 (*Letters*, II, p. 621; *Lettere*, II, p. 19).

affections are ordered, leading men to "loving God above all things and their neighbors as themselves."[24] Just as in the *Dialogue*, prudence is associated with charity. In letter 272 (which contains the first outline of the doctrine of the bridge, which Catherine would later develop in the *Dialogue*), Catherine affirms that the punishment owed to the conscience for having offended God should be guided with measure, yet flavored with the seasoning of charity, which makes the soul prudent.[25] It is then letter 353 that presents prudence in the fullness of its guiding role in the moral and spiritual life: it is in prudence, by the light of faith residing in the eye of our understanding, that "we look at what is harmful for us and what is beneficial" and, according to what we see, "we either love or despise."[26]

Prudence and discretion are jointly mentioned in letter 245, which addresses the theme of the self-love that weakens the will and leads to loving creatures outside of the will of God. It is only once the soul acquires the fortitude of the doctrine of the sweet and loving Word and of his blood that it knows and loves God by drowning its will in God's. It is this will, "vested with the sweet will of God," that makes us prudent and allows us to order our lives in wisdom and discretion:

> We love our Creator without measure and without intermediary. Not only do we not want to put created things or other people between ourselves and God; we don't even want to put ourselves—that is, our perverse selfish will—there. And just as we renounce ourselves, so we also renounce other people and all created things. I mean we do not love them apart from God'will, though we certainly do love them for God's sake. Our love, therefore, is well-ordered.[27]

---

24. *Letters*, III, p. 190 (*Lettere*, IV, pp. 138–39).
25. *Letters*, II, p. 500 (*Lettere*, IV, p. 165).
26. *Letters*, IV, p. 198 (*Lettere*, V, p. 199). See also *Letters*, III, pp. 306 and 308 (*Lettere*, V, pp. 127 and 130).
27. *Letters*, III, p. 107 (*Lettere*, IV, p. 49).

The will is free because it can choose between sin and virtue insofar as neither the devil nor any creature can force it to sin any more than it wants. Prudent people are happy in time of struggle because they realize that God allows this struggle to make them grow into greater and more proven virtue (letter 335);[28] and the prudent man, unlike the one who offends his Creator for the servile fear of displeasing creatures, runs to his mother (charity) and "feels secure and unafraid there" (letter 88).[29]

Prudence is also necessary in prayer. If we are prudent enough not to serve our own selfish will in the guise of consolation and not to believe the devil, but instead persevere in prayer in whatever way God grants it to us, we gain more in bitterness and pain than in sweetness (letter 71).[30] It is prudence, together with humility, that leads the soul from vocal prayer to mental prayer, which we attain when practicing vocal prayer prudently and humbly (letter 26).[31] So great is the importance that Catherine ascribes to prudence that, in writing to Urban VI in letter 370, she expresses her desire to see in him prudence with a sweet light of truth.[32]

Last, in letter 318, prudence is associated with wisdom in reference to God with a meaning similar to the one found in chapter 135 of the *Dialogue*:

> It would take too long to tell of everything there is to read in this book. But open your mind's eye by the light of most holy faith and redirect the feet of your affection to read this dearest of books. There you find prudence. There you find the wisdom with which Christ caught the devil on the hook of our humanity.[33]

28. *Letters*, II, p. 585 (*Lettere*, V, p. 105).
29. *Letters*, I, p. 228 (*Lettere*, II, p. 77).
30. *Letters*, II, p. 404 (*Lettere*, I, p. 71).
31. *Letters*, IV, pp. 193–94 (*Lettere*, I, pp. 87–88).
32. *Letters*, IV, p. 355 (*Lettere*, V, pp. 270–71).
33. *Letters*, IV, p. 106 (*Lettere*, V, p. 53).

4. DISCRETION AND LIGHT

As was mentioned before, it is undoubtedly difficult to interpret Catherine's language, which is rich with images used in a highly personal manner and abounding with repetitions and occasional imprecisions and inconsistencies. The image of the light is one example: it recurs often in Catherine's writings and is used in reference to a variety of concepts that, though, are presented in close relation to one another. Just to cite some of the more significant images in the *Letters*, one can find the "discreet light" or "light of discretion," the "light of reason," the "light of the intellect," the "light of faith," the "light of the Holy Spirit," the "light of grace," and the "light of truth."

How do the images of the light and the light of faith relate to the notion of discretion? In letter 213, the light of discretion or discreet light is first of all presented as true knowledge that, by showing man what he owes and to whom, guides all of his operations toward the just end of rendering the debt. Hence the discreet light is immediately set in relation to true knowledge. In letter 173, on the other hand, Catherine pauses at greater length on the image of the light, by writing that the virtue of discretion has its root in charity and is true knowledge of ourselves and of God: it has light because, without it, "its every principle and work would be imperfect."[34]

This light exists only when the pupil of faith sheds light on the eye of our intellect by allowing it to know the truth.[35] It is the eye of the intellect, enlightened by the light of faith, that enables us to understand the truth such that, when we come to see and know the truth, we love it, and with the light of discretion we can "judge rightly."[36] This same letter 307, addressed to a "woman who spoke ill," is about those who judge and condemn others while forgetting that, in the judgment by which we judge others, we will ourselves

---

34. *Letters*, II, p. 508 (*Lettere*, III, p. 78).
35. *Letters*, II, p. 507 (*Lettere*, III, p. 76).
36. *Letters*, III, p. 319 (*Lettere*, IV, p. 287).

be judged. These are people who wish to make themselves judges of the will of men, forgetting that it is the creature's place to be judged, not to judge. This happens because, not having the light of truth, they lightly pass judgment on what they have never seen and thus "become indiscreet."[37]

Again in letter 343, addressed to Raymond of Capua, Catherine insists at length on the true and most perfect light, which is the light of faith, and on what the soul that has this light does and which fruits it receives. Without this light, we would wander in darkness. The only way to escape darkness and obtain light is to set before the eyes of our intellect Christ crucified, a focal point that dries up the "dampness of selfish love" and allows us to take up "the knife of hatred for vice," which is discretion, and to love in proportion to our knowledge: "we love as much as we see, and our vision is perfect to the extent that the light is perfect."[38] It is solely the light of faith that leads us to know and love the truth because, as is written in letter 318:

> We love what we know as good, but without knowing it we cannot love it. And if we don't see it, we cannot know it. So we need the light. Without it we will be walking in darkness, and those who walk in darkness stumble.[39]

The saint calls this doctrine, in letter 315, "the wheel of the sun": God is the sun of justice "who enlightens everyone who wants to be enlightened by him. In his light we see light."[40] The light is necessary for traveling along the road of Christ crucified, a bright road that grants us life. As we know from letter 316, there are two ways in which it behooves us to have this light. The first one is the light (which everyone should have) that allows us to know "what we ought to love and whom we should obey." With the eye of understanding

37. *Letters*, III, p. 321 (*Lettere*, IV, p. 289).
38. *Letters*, IV, pp. 266–67 (*Lettere*, V, pp. 142–43).
39. *Letters*, IV, p. 103 (*Lettere*, V, pp. 50–51).
40. *Letters*, IV, p. 94 (*Lettere*, V, p. 32).

and its pupil, which is faith, we see that we are bound to love our Creator "with all our heart and all our might, unconditionally, and to obey the law that commands us to love God above all things and our neighbors as ourselves."[41]

In addition to this natural light to which we are all bound, since man would be deprived of a life of grace without it, there is another light, which is united to the first one and can be reached from the first one. In fact, those who obey God's commandments grow in another most perfect light: "they rise from imperfection and come to perfection by great and holy desire, observing the commandments and counsel both in mind and practice." We have to use this second light "with hungry desire for God's honor and the salvation of souls." Once we have come to know the truth in perfect light, we rise above ourselves and "run on in the footsteps of Christ crucified—with suffering, reproaches, derision, and insults."[42]

In letter 201, too, the theme of the two lights returns. Everyone is bestowed with a natural light, which is an imperfect light that God has granted us by nature, through which we know what is good. If one exercises this natural light with virtue, seeking out the good where it is, he perfects himself in the second light, which is supernatural, yet without leaving the first behind; rather, he rises from his imperfection and becomes perfect through the perfect supernatural light. This is because the first light sees the virtues, how pleasing they are to God and how beneficial for the soul, while the second light embraces the virtues and brings them to fruition in our charity for our neighbors.[43]

This distinction between natural or imperfect light and supernatural or perfect light is further articulated in letter 301. Natural light would always lead to knowing and choosing what is good if it were not covered by the cloud of self-love. It is therefore necessary

41. *Letters*, III, pp. 328–29 (*Lettere*, V, p. 38).
42. *Letters*, III, p. 329 (*Lettere*, V, pp. 38–39).
43. *Letters*, III, pp. 253–54 (*Lettere*, III, p. 183).

to exercise this light with attachment to the virtues so that we may achieve perfect knowledge: "with the help of this first and natural light, which is imperfect, we shall acquire a perfect light beyond the natural, infused into our soul by grace."[44]

Leading this reflection to its conclusion, Catherine identifies, in letter 64, not two but three lights, corresponding to the three degrees of perfection in knowing the truth, loving it, and practicing the virtues. The shared light or natural light is present when we come to recognize "the transitory things of the world" and our own weakness that leads us to rebel against the Creator.[45] But the soul needs to advance in perfection and acquire the perfect light, and this can be done in two ways. The first way, to which the second light corresponds, is the way of those who "devote themselves entirely to chastising their body by performing severe and enormous penances."[46] The second way, to which the third light corresponds, is the way of those who seek only the honor of God, arriving at the altar of the will of God, where the soul is entirely dead to its own will. At this point, their souls are in love and thirsting for love: "having completely drowned their own will in this light and knowledge, they shun no burden, from whatever source it may come."[47]

5. DISCRETION AND KNOWLEDGE

True knowledge lies at the heart of Catherine's spirituality. Without it, we cannot participate in divine grace. Knowledge is first of all knowledge of the "nothingness" of man, on the ontological plane, and of his sinfulness.[48] Acknowledging that man has received his

---

44. *Letters*, III, p. 334 (*Lettere*, IV, pp. 264–66).

45. *Letters*, III, p. 241 (*Lettere*, I, p. 238).

46. *Letters*, III, p. 242 (*Lettere*, I, p. 239).

47. *Letters*, III, p. 243 (*Lettere*, I, p. 241). See also *Letters*, III, p. 194 (*Lettere*, III, p. 134); *Letters*, III, p. 266 (*Lettere*, I, p. 171).

48. See, for example, letter 60: *Letters*, I, p. 115 (*Lettere*, I, p. 225).

being and all the graces on top of being from the "sweet goodness of God" leads to true humility because, in the words of letter 362, "we cannot be proud of what is nothing in and of itself."[49] In a certain sense, humility is the proof that knowledge of self has been achieved. Letter 197 speaks of "humility or true self-knowledge,"[50] showing the dependence of the two notions on one another.

Knowledge of self also involves knowledge of God, even though knowledge of self, as the "night of true knowledge," would seem to take precedence over knowledge of God, such as in letter 365, where Catherine warns Stefano di Corrado Maconi, her disciple, that, if his soul should prefer "to travel in the daytime of knowledge of God rather in the night of self-knowledge," he would be captured by his enemies. This is why she invites him "always to live between day and night" by coming to know himself in God and God in himself.[51] In letter 104, too, the saint seems to give precedence to the "night of self-knowledge, which is a sort of moonlight," after which comes "the day, with the great light and warmth of the sun."[52] At other times, such as in letters 70 and 317, precedence is instead given to the knowledge of God.[53]

Once the eye of understanding has discerned good from evil, the affection follows the intellect and quickly runs to love the Creator, recognizing his "indescribable love in the blood."[54] It is therefore the blood of Christ that manifests God's truth and charity.[55]

For Catherine, knowledge of God and knowledge of self in God are actually two inseparable aspects of the one true knowledge, which is true because it brings man to know God, who is Truth, and himself in God. Letter 226 presents the evocative image of God as a fountain:

49. *Letters*, IV, p. 222 (*Lettere*, V, p. 238).
50. *Letters*, II, p. 428 (*Lettere*, III, p. 165).
51. *Letters*, III, pp. 133–34 (*Lettere*, V, p. 253).
52. *Letters*, II, p. 654 (*Lettere*, II, p. 137).
53. *Letters*, I, p. 43 (*Lettere*, I, p. 266); *Letters*, IV, p. 6 (*Lettere*, V, p. 42).
54. Letter 80: *Letters*, III, p. 141 (*Lettere*, vol. II, p. 37).
55. See letter 102 (*Letters*, IV, p. 346; *Lettere*, II, p. 127); letter 193 (*Letters*, III, p. 90; *Lettere*, III, pp. 149–50); letter 279 (*Letters*, III, p. 210; *Lettere*, IV, p. 189).

Desire then disposes them to love themselves in God, and God in themselves, just as we, when we look into a fountain and see our image, take pleasure in it and love ourselves. But if we are wise, we are moved to love the fountain before we love ourselves. For if we hadn't seen ourselves we wouldn't have loved ourselves or taken pleasure in ourselves.[56]

In expressing the same concept, letter 369 makes use of the image of the house of knowledge of ourselves in which we find the fire of divine charity, as well as our wretchedness, ignorance, and ingratitude.[57] Just as the knowledge of self requires the knowledge of God, since man can only know himself by knowing himself in God, so, too, must humility and charity exist side by side because, if we know ourselves, "we humble ourselves, not holding our head high or becoming bloated with pride." As was recalled earlier, humility is the "governess and wet nurse" of charity, and without them both we cannot have life.[58]

The two virtues of humility and charity can only be acquired through true knowledge, as is clarified in letter 211.[59] True knowledge is the "cell of knowledge" of self and of the goodness of God in himself, as in letter 37. It is in this cell that we learn the virtues of humility and charity because in self-knowledge "we come to know how imperfect we are and that we are nothing." In it, we see that we have received our being from God and credit our Creator "for every grace we have received over and above our being. This is how we learn true and perfect charity."[60]

There are really two cells in one, because being in the cell of true knowledge of self also means finding oneself in the cell of the knowledge of the goodness of God. Hence being in one cell also implies the

56. *Letters*, II, p. 8 (*Lettere*, III, pp. 297–98).
57. *Letters*, IV, p. 337 (*Lettere*, V, p. 267).
58. Letter 177: *Letters*, II, p. 97 (*Lettere*, III, p. 91).
59. *Letters*, II, p. 168 (*Lettere*, III, p. 224).
60. *Letters*, III, p. 13 (*Lettere* I, p. 143).

need to be in the other; otherwise, the soul "would end up either in confusion or in presumption."[61] It is in living within the cell of knowledge that one finds the trinitarian God by means of the three faculties of the soul: memory, intellect, and will.[62] And it is in living within the same cell that we discover how man's ontological dependence on God implies also his dependence for knowledge.[63]

6. DISCRETION AND DEBT IN THE *LETTERS*

From the analysis of the *Letters*, and in particular letter 213, it clearly emerges that the role of discretion is not only that of showing, as light and knowledge, what should be given and to whom but also that of inducing a person to give in the most appropriate manner, such that all the operations of the soul are carried out with the purpose of rendering the debt. Since the latter is ultimately the primary role of discretion, it is now appropriate to examine several passages containing the term *debt*.

In letter 173, one reads that man grows in charity through the knowledge he has of himself and the knowledge of the goodness of God, and that charity, nurtured by humility, has at its side the child of true discretion, so that we discreetly

> pay our debt to God by giving glory and praise to his name. To ourselves we pay the debt of hatred and contempt for our selfish sensuality. And to our neighbors we give the kindness of loving them as we should, with a familial charity generous and well-ordered, not feigned or out of proportion.[64]

---

61. Letter 49: *Letters*, II, pp. 601–2 (*Lettere*, I, p. 191). See also letter 94 (*Letters*, II, p. 672; *Lettere*, II, p. 96) and letter 41, with the powerful image of the cell of the soul (*Letters*, I, p. 8; *Lettere*, I, p. 169). On this image, see G. Cavallini, *Things Visible and Invisible. Images in the Spirituality of St. Catherine of Siena* (Sr. M. Jeremiah, OP, tr.), New York, 1996, pp. 51–60.

62. Letter 241: *Letters*, II, p. 209 (*Lettere*, IV, pp. 34–35).

63. Letter 33: *Letters*, III, p. 272 (*Lettere*, I, p. 124).

64. *Letters*, II, p. 508 (*Lettere*, III, p. 77).

Catherine often contrasts grace and debt to emphasize, on the one hand, the infinite goodness of God, who made man in his image and likeness and recreated him in the blood of Christ out of grace and not out of debt, and, on the other hand, man who is obliged out of debt to love God and, because of this love, to love himself and his neighbor as well.[65]

There are many passages in the *Letters* that emphasize the infinite goodness of God, who has given us everything out of grace and not out of debt.[66] One of the recurring themes is the "price of blood" paid by Christ for the redemption of man, washing away the leprosy of our sins: he did so "in gratuitous mercy, and not because he had to."[67]

God's love for man is truly infinite.[68] At the same time, letter 164 reminds us that, even though God loves us unconditionally, freely, and generously out of grace and not out of debt, man cannot love God with that same love, with the consequence that we are "always obligated in duty to love," given as we are a share in God's goodness and blessings.[69] It is therefore essential to know, on the one hand, the great goodness of God and his ineffable charity toward us and, on the other hand, the perverse law that constantly attacks the spirit, and our wretchedness. Once we obtain this knowledge, as letter 266 indicates, "we begin to repay our debt of praise and glory to God by loving God above all things and our neighbors as ourselves."[70]

We therefore begin rendering the debt through true knowledge, and this knowledge is true because it brings us to know the truth that is what frees us: in knowing it we love it and in loving it we are freed from slavery to mortal sin. To this truth "we must pay the debt."[71] It

65. Letter 94: *Letters*, II, p. 668 (*Lettere*, II, pp. 90–91).
66. See, for example, letter 171 (*Letters*, II, p. 26; *Lettere*, III, p. 69) and also letter 27 (*Letters*, I, p. 310; *Lettere*, I, p. 92).
67. Letter 76: *Letters*, II, p. 622 (*Lettere*, II, p. 21). See also letter 248 (*Letters*, III, pp. 311–12; *Lettere*, IV, p. 59) and letter 345 (*Letters*, IV, p. 282; *Lettere*, V, p. 160).
68. See, for example, letter 101: *Letters*, II, p. 67; *Lettere*, II, p. 122.
69. *Letters*, II, p. 31 (*Lettere*, III, pp. 36–37).
70. *Letters*, III, pp. 187–88 (*Lettere*, IV, pp. 135–36).
71. Letter 48: *Letters*, IV, p. 134 (*Lettere*, I, p. 185).

DISCRETION IN THE *LETTERS*

is indeed impossible to participate in divine grace if this debt of love for God is not paid.[72] The soul, which through light and grace can see this debt that must be rendered, feels obliged to respond to God. When the devil and the soul's own weakness want to dissuade the soul from responding to God by whispering, "Why bother with this?," the soul should respond: because God "has commanded it and I owe it to him" and because I am obligated by grace "since it is by grace that I have received my existence and every gift over and above my existence." Therefore, had I not been commanded to do so, I would still be bound to do it because of the graces I have received.[73]

Ultimately, rendering the debt is an act of justice that every creature endowed with reason is called to perform.[74] Being just means precisely rendering one's debt to all. One reads in letter 357 that one of the signs by which the soul demonstrates its charitable state is when we give everyone what is due:

> To God we give glory, and we praise his name; to ourselves we give hatred and disgust for our sin; and to our neighbors we give love and benevolence. If we are in authority and have to mete out justice, we do right by everyone, the great as well as the small, the poor as well as the rich.[75]

But rendering the debt is more than an act of mere justice; it is an act of "holy justice," because it must be performed in accordance with charity. This is why "charity is never without justice (those who possess charity justly are in fact just),"[76] and why charity "is just in giving every person his or her due."[77] It is the remembrance of God's good

---

72. See letter 114: *Letters*, II, p. 341 (*Lettere*, II, p. 176).

73. Letter 354: *Letters*, IV, p. 246 (*Lettere*, V, pp. 207–8). See also letter 311: *Letters*, IV, pp. 307–8 (*Lettere*, V, pp. 3–4).

74. Letter 366: *Letters*, IV, p. 297 (*Lettere*, V, p. 259).

75. *Letters*, IV, p. 238 (*Lettere*, V, p. 220). See also letter 149 (*Letters*, I, pp. 61–62; *Lettere*, V, pp. 299–300) and letter 363 (*Letters*, IV, p. 315; *Lettere*, V, p. 247).

76. Letter 86: *Letters*, IV, p. 287 (*Lettere*, II, p. 69).

77. Letter 279: *Letters*, III, p. 210 (*Lettere*, IV, p. 190).

works and of his goodness that should lead us to accept all suffering for Jesus, with "a holy justice that will give every person what is justly due."[78]

7. CONCLUSION

In conclusion, the importance of rendering the debt reveals the essential role that discretion plays in the moral and spiritual life. Once light and knowledge have shown what must be given and to whom, all the operations of the soul are to be carried out with the one and only purpose of rendering the debt. This is therefore the primary act of discretion, which is also an act of justice informed by charity.

78. Letter 133: *Letters*, I, p. 124 (*Lettere*, II, pp. 250–51).

Chapter 7

A Final Step

Discretion in the Prayers

1. INTRODUCTION

It was mentioned before that the *Prayers*, unlike the *Dialogue* and the *Letters*, were not dictated by Catherine but were instead written by some of her disciples (perhaps even without her knowledge) while Catherine was absorbed in prayer. This peculiar origin of the *Prayers*, whereby one may suggest that, in a certain sense, they manifest the spontaneous expression of the saint's prayerful meditation, adds to their importance and the regret that such a scant number of them are available to us.

Obviously, the *Prayers* are examined here from the limited perspective of the passages where the term *discretion* and its synonym *prudence* occur. After this preliminary analysis, it will be possible to move on to identifying those passages where the expressions "light," "knowledge," and "rendering the debt" are linked, more or less directly, to discretion.

2. DISCRETION AND PRUDENCE IN THE *PRAYERS*

There are a few passages in the *Prayers* where discretion is presented under its name. In prayer 16, having contrasted the strength of the divine nature of the Word with the weakness of human nature, Catherine affirms that human nature has been strengthened by its union with the divinity of the Word and, when man reaches the age of discretion, he is further strengthened by Christ's teaching.[1] As was recalled earlier, in analyzing the *Letters*, the time of discretion is the age of reason when, having already received the gift of baptism and therefore the light of faith, man is called to exercise the virtues. The saint also speaks of discretion in prayer 18, one of her most beautiful prayers. In it, she turns to the Virgin Mary, asking that the pope be given light so that he may with discretion take the necessary steps to reform the Church.[2]

The term *prudence*, on the other hand, occurs in prayers 15, 17, and 18. In talking about a soul enlightened by God, the saint affirms in prayer 15 that in all things the soul exercises compassion prudently because it has seen how prudently God has worked his mysteries in us:

> You, Light, make the heart simple, not two-faced. You make it big, not stingy—so big that it has room in its loving charity for everyone: with well-ordered charity it seeks everyone's salvation, and because light is never without prudence and wisdom, it is ready to give its body up to death for the salvation of a neighbor's soul.[3]

In prayer 17, Catherine sees human beings as trees that are dead, due to original sin, and to whom life is provided by Christ through the "engrafting of divinity into humanity." In this manner the soul, engrafted into the Word in truth, becomes "faithful, prudent, patient."[4] Last, in prayer 18, Catherine invokes the Virgin who, having this light, was "prudent, not foolish." It was her prudence that made her want to

---

1. *Prayers*, 16, p. 169 (*Orazioni*, IX, pp. 98–100).
2. *Prayers*, 18, p. 194 (*Orazioni*, XI, p. 130).
3. *Prayers*, 15, p. 155 (*Orazioni*, VIII, pp. 86–88).
4. *Prayers*, 17, p. 180 (*Orazioni*, X, p. 112).

find out from the angel how what he had announced would come to pass. Her "prudent questioning" showed her deep humility.[5]

Despite these passages, the fact remains that discretion and prudence are not often mentioned in the *Prayers*. (Moreover, the reference to prudence in prayer 15 is applied to God, as in chapter 135 of the *Dialogue* and in letter 318, and therefore has a particular meaning and supernatural dimension.) But in a greater number of prayers the terms *light* and *knowledge* are applied to discretion.

3. DISCRETION, LIGHT, AND KNOWLEDGE

By now, it should have emerged clearly that knowledge plays a key role in Catherine's spirituality, a knowledge that is true because it involves knowledge of God (the "first sweet Truth") and knowledge of self in God. True knowledge can only be attained when natural reason is enlightened by faith in such a way that, unobstructed by self-love, it can see and know the truth and love it. In the *Prayers*, too, light is the principle of all true knowledge. Without this knowledge, the soul remains deprived of what constitutes a vital need: knowing and loving the truth. In prayer 15, the "sweet gentle light" is invoked as the principle and foundation of our health because in this light we see the eternal goodness of God, and knowing it we love it.[6] With regard to this light, the saint had observed that evil comes from darkness while good comes from the light, as "we cannot love what we do not know, and we can know nothing without the light."[7]

Moreover, to know, one needs to have the will to know. This is because, in Catherine's beautiful image, God's light stands at the soul's gate, and, as soon as the gate is opened to it, the light enters, "just like the sun that knocks at the shuttered window and, as soon as it is opened, comes into the house."[8]

5. *Prayers*, 18, pp. 187–88 (*Orazioni*, XI, pp. 120–22).
6. *Prayers*, 15, pp. 152–53 (*Orazioni*, VIII, p. 84).
7. *Prayers*, 15, p. 151 (*Orazioni*, VIII, p. 82).
8. *Prayers*, 15, p. 153 (*Orazioni*, VIII, pp. 84–86).

Man has been given the opportunity of knowing God and himself if the light of faith accompanies that light of reason with which he has been endowed by nature. The light of faith, which is indispensable for salvation, can only be exercised when one strips himself of his own will and allows to be vested by the divine will.[9] Only then can one be in the light, whereas one who vests himself in self-love is in darkness.[10] But God did not wish for man to wander in darkness, which is why he provided him with the light of faith.[11] To persevere in this light, one must oppose sensuality and seek to practice a virtuous life. Otherwise, even the natural light of reason ends up being lost.[12]

Natural reason alone is sufficient for man to recognize the divine image in himself, but the light of faith is necessary for a perfect knowledge of God, whereby man knows not only his ontological dependence on God but also the love that lies at the origin of creation and that became manifest in the incarnation of the Word.[13] For man to know himself and God, the Word became flesh and manifested the truth in his blood. God's greatest gift to his creature endowed with reason is having created man in his image and likeness, with the capacity to know and love God. This capacity is reflected in the structure of the human soul itself, in its three faculties: memory, intellect, and will. In prayer 17, man is seen as a "tree of life," to which his Creator gave the branches of memory (with the fruit of preserving), understanding (with the fruit of discerning), and will (with the fruit of loving).[14]

But after original sin this tree became a "tree of death." The Trinity, therefore, seeing that this tree could produce no fruit other than death, because it had become separated from God, provided the

9. *Prayers*, 12, pp. 111–12 (*Orazioni*, XXII, p. 250).

10. *Prayers*, 11, pp. 94–95 (*Orazioni*, XXI, p. 234).

11. *Prayers*, 14, p. 142 (*Orazioni*, VII, p. 72), and *Prayers*, 12, p. 114 (*Orazioni*, XXII, p. 254).

12. *Prayers*, 16, p. 170 (*Orazioni*, IX, p. 100).

13. *Prayers*, 13, pp. 124–6 (*Orazioni*, IV, pp. 38–40).

14. *Prayers*, 17, p. 175 (*Orazioni*, X, p. 106). See *Prayers*, 4, p. 40 (*Orazioni*, XXIII, p. 264), and *Prayers*, 22, pp. 236–37 (*Orazioni*, XVII, p. 196).

remedy by grafting divinity into the dead tree of our humanity so that, as Catherine continues in the same prayer, when we have been grafted into God, the branches begin to produce their fruit:

> Our memory is filled with the continual recollection of your [i.e. God's] blessings. Our understanding gazes into you to know perfectly your truth and your will. And our will chooses to love and to follow what our understanding has seen and known. So each branch offers its fruit to the others. And because of our knowledge of you we know ourselves better and hate ourselves—I mean we hate our selfish sensuality.[15]

Having been enlightened by the true light, the soul can see that God has made us the gift of fashioning us after his image and likeness, sharing himself as Trinity in the soul's three faculties or powers. Once enlightened, the soul can also see itself dwelling in God by following his "Truth's teaching."[16]

The two verbs *to see* and *to know* are correlative to the two terms *light* and *knowledge*, often referring to the role of discretion in discerning the truth. In turn, the attainment of knowledge and the will to act upon it are linked to the harmonious unity of the three faculties of memory, intellect, and will.[17] While the memory has the task of preserving and showing God's good works (i.e. showing them to the intellect), it is the intellect that sees and knows them in the light. Both seeing and knowing come from the intellect, which in turn moves the will to love what it has seen and known. Ultimately, the "sweet and gentle light" is truly the "principle and foundation of our health" because, as Catherine affirms in prayer 15, it is in the light that God saw our need, and it is in this same light that we see his eternal goodness, "and knowing it we love it."[18]

---

15. *Prayers*, 17, pp. 177–78 (*Orazioni*, X, pp. 108–10).
16. *Prayers*, 11, pp. 98–99 (*Orazioni*, XXI, p. 238).
17. *Prayers*, 17, p. 179 (*Orazioni*, X, p. 112), and *Prayers*, 12, p. 116 (*Orazioni*, XXII, p. 256).
18. *Prayers*, 15, pp. 152–53 (*Orazioni*, VIII, p. 84).

It has been stressed in this study more than once that the recognition of the ontological dependence of human beings on God lies at the root of Catherine's spirituality. Man depends on God not only for his being but also for his knowledge of the truth. *Being* means participating in the being of God, so knowing the truth means participating in the truth that is God. As being and truth in God are identical, and as man depends on God both in his being and in his knowledge, man can only exist by way of participation and can likewise only know the truth by way of participation. This leads Catherine to exclaim in prayer 21:

> Truth! Truth! And who am I that you give me your truth? I am the one who is not. It is your truth then that does and speaks and accomplishes all things, because I am not. It is your truth that offers truth, and with your truth I speak the truth....You, Godhead eternal, God's Son, came from God to fulfill the eternal Father's truth. No one can possess truth except from you, Truth. And those who want to possess your truth must have *all* of your truth; in no other way can they possess the truth, which cannot be less than complete.[19]

4. DISCRETION AND DEBT IN THE *PRAYERS*

In the *Prayers*, as in the *Dialogue* and the *Letters*, paying the debt is the primary act of discretion, namely the rendering of the debt to God, self, and neighbor.

Catherine's typical approach is setting grace in opposition to debt, such as in prayer 11, where Catherine stresses that God loves the soul gratuitously, having loved the soul before it came to be, while the soul loves God out of duty. On the other hand, the soul's love for neighbor is both gratuitous and out of duty: the soul loves the neighbors gratuitously because it does not search for any return from them, and it

---

19. *Prayers*, 21, p. 232 (*Orazioni*, XV, p. 180).

loves them out of duty because God commands it and it is the soul's duty to obey God.[20] The accent of this prayer is on the need to submit one's own will to God's because it is only in the divine light that the soul allows itself to be vested with the will of God. A soul vested with self-love instead finds itself in darkness.[21]

The reference to grace and debt occurs also in prayer 15,[22] while the theme of the gratuitousness of creation and of the redemption carried out by the Word returns in prayer 1.[23] These passages are additional to those where debt is mentioned only implicitly, such as in prayer 17, where one reads that memory reminds us that we are bound (hence have a debt) to love God and follow the teaching and example of his only-begotten Son.[24]

5. CONCLUSION

This analysis of the *Prayers* confirms that Catherine often applies the terms *light* and *knowledge*, together with the verbs *to see* and *to know*, to discretion in its function of discerning the truth. This emphasizes also the importance of the three faculties of the soul through which man can come to know and love the truth. In Catherine's reflection, memory has the task of preserving the good works of God, which is to say "being and all the gifts bestowed on top of being," and of showing them to the intellect. Vivified by the light, the intellect in turn moves the will to love what it has seen and known. Hence both seeing and knowing come from the intellect.

The analysis of the *Prayers* has also confirmed the crucial role of the knowledge of truth for salvation; this truth has been defined as "the hallmark of the life, thought and style of Saint Catherine."[25]

20. *Prayers*, 11, pp. 99–100 (*Orazioni*, XXI, p. 240).
21. *Prayers*, 11, pp. 102–3 (*Orazioni*, XXI, p. 244).
22. *Prayers*, 15, pp. 157–58 (*Orazioni*, VIII, p. 90).
23. *Prayers*, 1, p. 8 (*Orazioni*, I, p. 12).
24. *Prayers*, 17, p. 179 (*Orazioni*, X, p. 112).
25. This is what G. Cavallini writes in her introduction to the *Dialogo*, at p. xxxi.

Being is closely connected with knowing, by virtue of which connection man depends on God not only for his being but also for his knowledge of the truth, insofar as being and truth are identical in God. Ultimately, just as one can only exist by way of participation, so one can only know the truth by way of participation. This accounts for Catherine's affirmation, when addressing God ("You are the One who is but I am the one who is not"), which seems to communicate not only her profound recognition of man's ontological dependence on God, but also man's dependence on God for knowing the truth.

* * *

The purpose of this second part was to analyze Catherine's writings with a view to determining the meaning and role of discretion. In carrying out this task, annoying repetitions could not be avoided. The fact, though, is that an inventory of Catherine's relevant passages would not have been complete without accepting the risk of repetition, precisely because, to Catherine, repeating herself was insignificant: what counted for her was substance (not form), namely the search for the truth irrespective of any stylistic awkwardness (or at least what may sound so to the contemporary reader) or, at the opposite, the beauty of her incisive images (on account of which she has always been ranked as a towering figure in Italian literature).

In examining the *Dialogue*, the focus in this part was on the relationship between discretion and the virtues that constitute the milestones of Catherine's spiritual itinerary. The starting point was true knowledge, attained by the light of faith through the discovery of the infinite abyss between the nothingness of man—his ontological dependence on God and the moral wretchedness of sin—and the everything of God and God's infinite love. It is this true knowledge that leads man into the valley of humility and charity by assessing exactly what man is in comparison to God. Immersed in charity, the soul experiences hatred for and aversion to its own sins and longs to pay its debt to God, itself, and its neighbor. In its guiding role, discretion not only shows man the most suitable manner of paying this debt but also drives him to do so. On the one hand, discretion is a form of discernment derived from the true knowledge of what man owes God, himself, and his neighbor; on the other hand, it is more than discernment, in that it also inspires him to act in accordance with this practical knowledge and leads to its concrete fulfillment, thus constituting the unifying condition for moral and spiritual life as a whole.

Then, the study of the *Letters*, starting from letter 213, allowed the investigation of discretion (and prudence, its synonym) in its relationship with light, knowledge, and debt, highlighting the role of discretion in discerning the truth. Within this context, rendering the debt emerged as the primary act of discretion because, once light and knowledge have shown what must be given and to whom, all of the operations of the soul must be carried out with the one and only purpose of rendering the debt.

The analysis of the *Prayers* confirmed the identical meaning of discretion and prudence in Catherine's writings (except for the cases where prudence is used in reference to God, in prayer 15, letter 318, and chapter 135 of the *Dialogue*) and also the link between discretion-prudence and the terms *light–to see* and *knowledge–to know*. Moreover, the examination of the three faculties (memory, intellect, and will) showed that both seeing and knowing, which represent discretion as discernment of the truth, come from the intellect, the noblest aspect of the soul that is moved by the will and in turn nourishes it. The will, in turn, is "love's hand" and fills the memory with thoughts of God and of his blessings.[26]

In conclusion, this analysis has evidenced that discretion is the condition for a unified moral and spiritual life because it unites discernment, which is derived from the knowledge and love of the truth, with its practical fulfillment in the virtuous action, namely in the harmonious unity of the three faculties (memory, intellect, and will): "So each power lends a hand to the other, thus nourishing the soul in the life of grace."[27]

---

26. *Dialogue*, p. 103, ch. 51 (*Dialogo*, p. 135).
27. Ibid.

PART III

COMPARISON IN HISTORICAL PERSPECTIVE

The Origins of Catherine's Discretion: From the Tradition of *Discretio* and Prudence to the Synthesis of Thomas Aquinas and the Reflections by Some of Catherine's Contemporaries

This part addresses the complex question of the origins of the notion of discretion in Catherine's writings, and does so in three chapters.

Chapter 8 addresses the Christian tradition of discretio spirituum and discretio that preceded Thomas Aquinas's synthesis of this tradition with Aristotle's teaching on prudence. While it is possible to find, in Catherine's writings, the meaning of discernment in the sense of discretio spirituum, Catherine's notion is much closer to discretio, which, beginning with Cassian, came to be considered the mother of all virtues. For this reason, this chapter mentions only briefly the discretio spirituum and focuses instead on selected Christian writers who, before Aquinas, had dealt with discretio in its integral sense, encompassing the meaning not only of discernment of the spirits but also of measure.

Chapter 9 then addresses the tradition of prudence and considers summarily Thomas Aquinas's treatise on the virtue of prudence in the Summa Theologica (IIa–IIae, questions 47 to 56). As the terms discretion and prudence are synonyms in Catherine's writings, this chapter compares Aquinas's prudence with Catherine's discretion and prudence.

Finally, Chapter 10 considers a lesser yet important source of Catherine's discretion, namely Domenico Cavalca's Lo Specchio della Croce ("The Mirror of the Cross"). The same chapter briefly examines some writings of three of Catherine's contemporaries (Bridget of Sweden, John Colombini, and Raymond of Capua), with a view to comparing their use of the terms discretion and prudence with that of Catherine.

Chapter 8

A Brief Sketch of the Tradition of *Discretio* (Including *Discretio Spirituum*)

1. INTRODUCTION

In classical Latin, the terms *discernere* and *discretio* have the physical meaning of dividing, separating, and distinguishing, as well as the intellectual meaning of discerning and judging.[1] The same can be said of the corresponding Greek terms *diakrínein* and *diákrisis*.[2]

The idea of intellectual discernment—discernment between good and evil or true and false—can already be found in Plato and the Stoics. Nonetheless, despite a certain undeniable influence of the Stoics on early Christian writers, it seems that the latter essentially borrowed the word *discretio* from the Bible as the primary source of their thinking. The term *diakrínein* appears in the Greek version of the Old Testament at least twenty-five times, corresponding to the Hebrew roots of *schafat* or *rib*, whose Latin translations are *iudicare* or *discernere*, meaning "render justice," which involves a judgment or discernment. For example, the term in question is found in 1 Kings 3:9 on discernment between good and evil.

---

1. See the two terms in P. G. W. Glare (ed.), *Oxford Latin Dictionary*, Oxford, 1968, vol. 1, pp. 549–50 (*"discerno"*) and p. 551 (*"discretio"*).
2. See the two terms in H. G. Liddel and R. Scott (eds.), *A Greek-English Lexicon* (9th edn.), Oxford, 1996, p. 399.

The term *diákrisis* appears three times in the New Testament. In the Latin version, Saint Jerome translates it with the word *discretio* in Hebrews 5:14 and in 1 Corinthians 12:10 and with the word *disceptatio* in Romans 14:1. In Hebrews 5:14, the expression "*excitatos habent sensus ad discretionem boni ac mali*" refers to a practical intellectual attitude toward the discernment of doctrines, while *discretio spirituum* is listed among the charisms in 1 Corinthians 12:10, as an infused gift of grace. Based on meaning, the translation "*disceptatio cogitationum*" in Romans 14:1 is generally coupled with Hebrews 5:14.

In the language of the Church Fathers, the term *discretio* is used in the sense of discernment of the spirits and refers primarily to the ability to distinguish that which comes from God from that which does not come from him. When the first Christian writers began talking about the discernment of good and evil, they took their inspiration from the Bible, specifically from Saint Paul.[3] Therefore, it was initially the *discretio spirituum*, as the discernment of good and evil, that was found in the Christian tradition and then underwent a process of gradual development. This development was due to an ever deeper understanding of the inner movements of the soul: it was no longer merely distinguishing what came from God and what came from the devil but also discerning the most hidden thoughts and intentions of human beings in the spiritual struggle between good and evil.

According to Daniélou, this doctrine of the discernment of the spirits, which appeared for the first time in *The Shepherd of Hermas*, was turned by Clement of Alexandria into a standard component of Christian teaching. Through Origen, it then reached Athanasius, who made it the fundamental theme of his *Life of Saint Anthony*, before it was significantly developed by Evagrius Ponticus.[4] The notion of discernment of the spirits is also present in the theology of Saint

---

3. F. Dingjan, *Discretio*, op. cit., pp. 8–10.
4. See J. Daniélou, "Démon," in *Dictionnaire de Spiritualité* 3 (1957), cols. 152–89, at col. 168. On the evolution of the concept of discernment of the spirits in the Fathers of the Church before Cassian's time, see F. Dingjan, *Discretio*, op. cit., pp. 235–50.

Augustine, for example, in the reflections on the tree of knowledge of good and evil in his commentary on Genesis against the Manichees.[5] His passage regarding the two cities is much more famous, though: it is discernment that leads to true knowledge of self and of God and to distinguishing the city of God from the city of the demons.[6]

Discretio, understood as a moral virtue, derives from this older tradition of *discretio spirituum*.[7] As was mentioned before, the meaning of discernment in the sense of *discretio spirituum* is also present in Catherine's writings, for example, in the passage in the *Dialogue* where Catherine warns that the devil may present himself under the guise of an angel or a saint to deceive a soul. How can one discern whether this "visitation" comes from God or from the devil? For Catherine, the sign is this:

> If it is the devil who has come to visit the mind under the guise of light, the soul experiences gladness at his coming. But the longer he stays, the more gladness gives way to weariness and darkness and pricking as the mind becomes clouded over by his presence within. But when the soul is truly visited by me [i.e. God], eternal Truth, she experiences holy fear at the first encounter. And with this fear comes gladness and security, along with a gentle prudence.[8]

Catherine often speaks of the devil. In letter 84, which is addressed to two friars, Catherine dwells with the different varieties of devil's malice: he may openly discourage us from persevering in what is good

5. Augustine, *Two Books on Genesis against the Manichees and on the Literal Interpretation of Genesis: An Unfinished Book* (R. J. Teske tr.), Washington, DC, 1991, book ii, chs. 9, 12, 25, and 38.

6. Augustine, *Concerning the City of God against the Pagans* (J. O'Meara, ed., H. Bettenson, tr.), London, 1984, book xiv, ch. 28, pp. 593–94.

7. "In the studies on ancient and Medieval spirituality, not enough attention is paid to this evolution of the discernment of the spirits into discretion as a moral virtue" (F. Dingjan, "La pratique de la discrétion d'après les Lettres de Sainte Catherine de Sienne," op. cit., p. 15, note 47).

8. *Dialogue*, p. 133, ch. 71 (*Dialogo*, p. 185). On the discernment of visions, see also chs. 102 and 106, and what is written in *Life*, pp. 77–78, paras. 84–85.

or in enduring the hardship of obedience, but he may also resort to the subtle tactics of showing us the truth and leading us to recognize it, "but then, from behind," may attach "a lie that produces the venom of discouragement."[9] Only a "discreet" soul can defend itself against the devil (with his deceptions, misleading thoughts, and temptations) and the two other components of the perverse triad of the soul's primary enemies: the world with its vanities and delights and the appetite of the senses that desires inordinately.[10]

While it cannot be denied that discernment as *discretio spirituum* is present in Catherine's writings, in her spirituality, discretion has a much closer meaning to the *discretio* of that tradition that started with Cassian. Consequently, the starting point of this analysis is this author, who seems to have been the first one to use the word *discretio* not only in the sense of discernment of the spirits but also in the sense of virtue, thus injecting into the term the very meaning that would later identify the function of prudence.[11]

2. JOHN CASSIAN

The spiritual teachings of Cassian[12] are primarily addressed to monks with the intention of showing them the way to attain perfection.

---

9. *Letters*, IV, p. 211 (*Lettere*, II, pp. 54–55).

10. Letter 154: *Letters*, IV, p. 49 (*Lettere*, III, p. 6). The other letters where Catherine writes of the three enemies of the soul are 28, 36, 56, 62, 84, 88, 90, 96, 114, 128, 148, 159, 182, 183, 197, 201, 211, 215, 217, 220, 232, 245, 249, 254, 256, 257, 258, 259, 264, 266, 267, 272, 273, 275, 276, 278, 286, 287, 293, 294, 297, 299, 301, 304, 308, 309, 320, 331, 332, 334, 335, 343, 344, 345, 348, 353, 354, 356, 357, 358, 360, 365, 372, 374, 376, 377, 378, and 380.

11. "Discretion found in him an excellent theoretician. Later writers of ascetics repeat his teaching, without adding much to it" (A. Cabassut, "Discrétion," in *Dictionnaire de Spiritualité* 3 (1957), cols. 1311–30, at col. 1320). According to F. Dingjan, Cassian, as the first theoretician of *discretio*, widened and systematized what had been written by the Fathers of the desert, whose experiences Cassian described (*Discretio*, op. cit., p. 6, note 1).

12. On John Cassian (circa 360–435), see O. Chadwick, *John Cassian* (2nd edn.), Cambridge, 1968; A. M. C. Casiday, *Tradition and Theology in St John Cassian*, Oxford

For Cassian, discernment is first of all a function of the intellect that reflects upon the inner life of man to distinguish between good and evil. The criterion for this judgment is the end, because it is the end that gives meaning to all that is done to achieve it. In his first conference,[13] Cassian distinguishes the ultimate end (*finis*) from that which is done to attain it, or intermediate end (*scopos*), clarifying that the end of monastic life is the kingdom of God and that the intermediate end for attaining it is purity of heart (*puritas cordis*). Purity of heart means purification of all that is opposed to reaching the kingdom of God: vices but also anything that is useless for attaining the ultimate end. This is its negative aspect. In its positive aspect, purity of heart consists in charity.

The virtues and various forms of ascesis are merely means of perfection, intermediate ends the goodness of which depends essentially on their proportionality to the ultimate end in the various circumstances in which one is called to fulfill one's ultimate vocation.[14] Since man's ultimate end is contemplation of God, he must guard against anything that can disturb the purity and tranquility of the soul.[15] Therefore, it is first of all necessary to keep watch over the many and often conflicting thoughts passing through the soul.[16] Since good and evil actions have their origins in thoughts, discernment of them is indispensable for attaining purity of heart.

According to Cassian, there are three sources of thoughts: God, the devil, and man. Good thoughts are inspired by God; the devil works to provoke the fall of man by enticing him with the seduction of vices, often presenting evil in the form of good and transforming himself from time to time into an angel of light; last, thoughts have

---

and New York, 2007. On discretion in Cassian's reflection, see R. Appel, "Cassian's *Discretio*—A Timeless Virtue," *American Benedictine Review* 17 (1966), pp. 20–29.

13. J. Cassian, *The Conferences* (B. Ramsey, ed.), Mahwah, NJ, 1997, conference 1, pp. 35–75.

14. Ibid., conference 21, xiv, pp. 729–31.

15. Ibid., conference 1, vii, pp. 45–46.

16. Ibid., conference 1, v, pp. 43–44.

their origin in man as a result of the natural interplay of his faculties and are sometimes caused by negligence or evil will.[17] Nevertheless, even when the origin of the thoughts does not depend entirely on man, it is up to him to accept or reject them.[18] To do this, it is necessary to act with wise discretion (*sagaci discretione*). The author compares this task to that of a money-changer, who examines the coins and rejects the false ones with his most prudent discretion (*prudentissima discretione*).[19]

Cassian identifies four applications of the doctrine of discernment to the spiritual life. First, wise discretion is necessary for discerning among the various philosophies or heresies that often hide behind the mask of religion. Second, one must guard against false interpretations of the Scriptures. Third, one must beware of immoderate virtues because the devil sometimes incites man to perform immoderate actions under the guise of virtue, such as excessive fasting or vigils. Moreover, one who exercises the discernment of the spirits should not allow himself to be led astray by the devil, who provokes him to act without moderation to divert him from his end.[20] Fourth, discernment must be used regarding the honesty of actions, which are to be carried out with a view to giving glory to God and contributing to the common good, and not that of asserting one's vainglory.[21]

In the greater part of his first conference, Cassian refers to *discretio* as discernment of the spirits; it is only toward the end that he introduces *discretio* in the sense of measure, stating that it excels among the virtues as the mother of all measure (*moderationis generatrix*).[22]

17. Ibid., conference 1, xix, pp. 57–59.
18. Ibid., conference 1, xvii, p. 56.
19. Ibid., conference 1, xx, p. 59.
20. Ibid., conference 1, xx, p. 60.
21. Ibid., conference 1, xxii, pp. 62–63.
22. Ibid., conference 1, xxiii, pp. 63–64. The idea of measure and moderation is also present in such other authors as Saint Jerome and Saint Augustine, who, however, do not link it to *discretio*. In their reflection, the term *discretio* is used in a physical sense (separation) or an intellectual sense (discernment), but not in a moral sense (moderation) (F. Dingjan, *Discretio*, op. cit., p. 79, note 3).

In the second conference, after having explicitly referred to 1 Corinthians 12:10 to stress the charismatic aspect of the discernment of the spirits as a gift from the Holy Spirit (a grace that can only come from God),[23] Cassian illustrates by way of example how the fall of several characters was caused by a lack of *discretio*, a virtue he calls the "source and root of all the virtues."[24] No virtue can be acquired or maintained without discretion, because discretion is the "begetter, guardian, and moderator of all virtues."[25] It is *discretio* that directs the virtues along the path that leads to the perfection of charity by fulfilling the necessary conditions for human acts to attain this end. Among the different means, discretion distinguishes between those that are good and those that must be avoided, though presenting themselves under the guise of goodness.

Cassian also refers to *discretio* as the "light" or "eye of the body."[26] In ancient Greek tradition and also in the Judaic world, the eye not only sees the light of the sun but also captures this light and shines it on things, revealing them for what they are.[27] For Cassian, *discretio* is for the soul what the eye is for the body since it discerns all of man's thoughts and actions, examining and seeing in the light what needs to be done. He therefore affirms, citing Matthew 6:22-23, that, if the eye—which is like a lamp that shines and gives light—no longer gives light, one is left in darkness.[28]

Therefore, in Cassian's reflection, the concept of *discretio* entails two meanings: discernment of the spirits and measure. If it is true that the discernment of the spirits is the condition for *discretio* as measure, it is nonetheless in the moderation of actions that *discretio* reveals its full importance. In other words, if the discernment of good and evil thoughts and good and evil intentions is necessary,

---

23. J. Cassian, *The Conferences*, op. cit., conference 2, i, pp. 83–84.
24. Ibid., conference 2, ix, p. 90.
25. Ibid., conference 2, iv, p. 87.
26. Ibid., conference 2, ii, iii, and iv, pp. 85–86.
27. F. Dingjan, *Discretio*, op. cit., p. 31.
28. J. Cassian, *The Conferences*, op. cit., conference 2, ii, p. 85.

what ultimately counts is the upright fulfillment of what has been recognized as right; it is only in action, avoiding imbalance and acting with measure, that *discretio* is realized.

When comparing Cassian's to Catherine's *discretio*, it is not difficult to find points of commonality between the two. For example, the notion of "time of discretion" is present both in Catherine's writings[29] and in those of Cassian.[30] Likewise, Cassian sometimes calls *discretio* "light" and "lamp," and this recalls the aspect of "light" (*lume*) that discretion has in Catherine. Likewise, Cassian's view of immoderate fasting and penance, which should be regulated by *discretio*[31] since ascesis is only a means of attaining perfection and not the end itself, is similar to Catherine's. In letter 213, she writes that it is "the rule of discretion" that should determine a suitable penance, which is only an instrument for perfection. This, however, does not detract from the importance that Catherine places on fighting one's passion of the senses to attain an understanding of truth and the ability to judge with discretion: for her, the virtue of discretion is "the knife that kills and cuts off all selfish love to its foundation in self-will."[32]

Affirming that there is no discretion, and therefore no virtue, without a will that is guided by knowledge of oneself in God is equivalent to Cassian's doctrine on purity of heart as a necessary condition for the exercise of discretion.

In the end, the most significant similarity between Catherine and Cassian is the importance they both attribute to the reflection of the intellect on the inner life of man for the purpose of distinguishing good from evil. For Cassian, the ability to discern one's thoughts with "sagacious discretion" is indispensable for acquiring that "purity of heart" that is necessary to attain the kingdom of God. Furthermore, "true discretion" can only be acquired by paying the price of "true

---

29. As was mentioned earlier, Catherine refers to the age or time of discretion in letters 58, 199, and 215 and in prayer 16.

30. On this point, see F. Dingjan, *Discretio*, op. cit., p. 16.

31. J. Cassian, *The Conferences*, op. cit., conference 2, v, p. 87, and xvii, p. 100.

32. *Dialogue*, p. 43, ch. 11 (*Dialogo*, p. 33).

humility."[33] The same relevance of inner reflection is found in Catherine's "true knowledge," which is the basis for her entire spirituality and the fundamental requirement for discretion. As was seen in the second part of this study, the first step on Catherine's spiritual itinerary is true knowledge, which consists in knowledge of self and of God. It is from the knowledge of man's ontological nothingness and the moral wretchedness of sin, on the one hand, and of the divine "everything" and the infinite love of God, on the other, that humility emerges, giving an accurate assessment of what man is in comparison to God. For Catherine, as was stressed earlier in this study, humility derives from man's profound awareness of being nothing in himself, insofar as he receives being and all the gifts bestowed on top of being from God.

The close link between humility and discretion, which is present in Cassian, is a defining feature also of Catherine's spirituality: without humility, there is spiritual confusion and darkness, because man has wanted "to climb before descending."[34]

Finally, according to Cassian, *discretio* does not intervene only in the discernment of good and evil thoughts but also in the fulfillment of what has been recognized as right. This is because it is only in the moral act, avoiding imbalances and acting in accordance with right measure and moderation, that *discretio* is fulfilled. This combination of discernment and concrete moral action is also a clear aspect of Catherine's reflection: for her, once true knowledge has shown man what he must give and to whom, all the operations of the soul must be carried out with the one and only aim of rendering the debt.

---

33. J. Cassian, *The Conferences*, op. cit., conference 2, x, p. 90. (See also xvi, p. 99.)

34. Letter 343: *Letters*, IV, p. 268 (*Lettere*, V, p. 144). These are the other letters where this connection between knowledge and humility is stressed: 2, 4, 17, 23, 32, 33, 37, 38, 47, 49, 51, 61, 65, 75, 79, 81, 82, 83, 84, 108, 109, 113, 114, 141, 154, 169, 173, 177, 178, 185, 189, 190, 197 (in this letter, humilty is identified with the "true knowledge of self"), 211, 216, 221, 223, 224, 230, 234, 246, 250, 307, 310, 315, 317, 334, 335, 346, 351, 352, 353, 360, 362, 363, 366, and 369.

3. SAINT BENEDICT

Saint Benedict,[35] in his *Rule*,[36] addresses those aspiring to perfection who are seeking to attain it through the cenobitic life, which he considers the ideal form of monastic life.

Benedict's teachings are based on his personal experiences and his knowledge of earlier monastic literature.[37] Having a profound sense of tradition, this saint did not consider himself the founder of a new religious order but rather the father of a community to which he would transmit the wisdom of the monastic tradition passed down by others. His *Rule* was so successful, not so much on account of any search for originality, but precisely because it was seen as a masterful compendium of earlier monastic experience.[38]

Although the term *discretio* is found only three times in the *Rule*, twice in chapter 64 and once in chapter 70, the sense of balance and measure is so thoroughly recognized throughout Benedict's teachings

35. On Saint Benedict (circa 480–547), see A. de Vogüé, *Saint Benedict: The Man and His Work* (G. Malsbary, tr.), Petersham, MA, 2006. The main source on Benedict's life is Gregory the Great, *The Life of St. Benedict* (A. de Vogüé, ed., H. Costello and E. de Bhaldraithe, tr.), Petersham, MA, 1993.

36. For the Latin text and English translation of the *Rule*, see T. Fry (ed.), *RB 1980: The Rule of St. Benedict in Latin and English with Notes*, Collegeville, MN, 1980. For commentary, see A. de Vogüé, *The Rule of Saint Benedict: A Doctrinal and Spiritual Commentary* (J. B. Hasbrouck, tr.), Kalamazoo, MI, 1983.

37. The reference here is not only to his knowledge of the monastic tradition but also to the possibile dependence of Benedict's *Rule* from the *Regula Magistri*, a monastic rule written in Latin whose author is unknown. F. Dingjan has observed that the terms *discretio* and *prudentia* and the expression "*mater virtutum*" do not occur in the *Regula Magistri*; moreover, while the terms *mensura* and *modus* are present in several passages, they are never the subject of the virtue of discretion (*Discretio*, op. cit., p. 86, note 1). For an English translation of the *Regula Magistri*, see *The Rule of the Master. Regula Magistri* (A. de Vogüé, ed., L. Eberle and C. Philippi, tr.), Kalamazoo, MI, 1977. For a table of correspondences between the two rules, see T. Fry (ed.), *RB 1980*, op. cit., pp. 478–93.

38. "The Western monastic fathers were profoundly conscious of being heirs of a past, of a tradition. Their aim was not to produce something new but to collect, assimilate and propagate the monastic wisdom accumulated by their Eastern and Western predecessors. That wisdom was common property; there was no sense of literary authorship" (T. Fry (ed.), *RB 1980*, op. cit., p. 84).

that it was discretion that was indicated since the very beginning as the main characteristic of the *Rule*. About forty years after the death of the saint from Nursia, Pope Gregory the Great described the *Rule* as "remarkable for its discretion" (*discretione praecipuam*),[39] indirectly confirming that by the sixth century *discretio* was already a notion sufficiently well defined to have been applied to characterizing a set of practical directives.

Of the two chapters of the *Rule* in which the term *discretio* occurs, chapter 64 is devoted to the election of an abbot. The candidate is recommended to be moderate, "bearing in mind the discretion of holy Jacob."[40] The next verse states that the abbot, profiting from this and other similar examples of discretion, mother of all the virtues, must temper all things so that "the strong have something to yearn for and the weak nothing to run from."[41] Employing Cassian's definition of *discretion* as the "mother of all the virtues," Saint Benedict does not limit himself to requiring that discretion moderate the exercise of the abbot's authority; he also provides the criterion for it, thereby demonstrating great psychological depth.

In chapter 70, the term *discretio* is applied to the measure that should inspire one's conduct toward the others depending on differences in age. Those who are younger than fifteen years of age should be monitored by everyone, yet those who treat them "unreasonably" or without discretion (*sine discretione*) should in turn be subjected to the discipline of the rule.[42]

In conclusion, while discretion is considered above all the indispensable attribute of an abbot, whose task it is to interpret and apply

39. Saint Gregory the Great, *Dialogues* (O. J. Zimmerman, tr.), New York, 1959, ii, para. 36, p. 107. On account also of this judgment, Edith Stein (Saint Teresa Benedicta of the Cross, copatroness of Europe with Saints Catherine of Siena and Bridget of Sweden) identified discretion as the main feature of Benedictine holiness. (See J. Healy, "Edith Stein. *Sancta discretio*," *American Benedictine Review* 52 (2001), pp. 121–37, at p. 132.)

40. T. Fry (ed.), *RB 1980*, op. cit., ch. 64, verse 18, p. 283.

41. Ibid., ch. 64, verse 19, p. 283.

42. Ibid., ch. 70, p. 293.

the established rules, the numerous references to the measure that must be kept by all those who are subject to his authority prove that they, too, should have discretion—as the virtue of a just middle that avoids excesses—in the exercise of their respective roles. This sense of balance and measure that pervades all of Benedict's teachings, and for which his *Rule* has been described as *"discretione praecipuam,"* is quite close to Catherine's discretion, which is so encompassing that, in Catherine's own words, every time is the appropriate time and every place is the appropriate place.[43]

4. SAINT GREGORY THE GREAT

Influenced by the tradition that preceded him, particularly by Saint Augustine and Cassian, Saint Gregory[44] posits the union of action with contemplation as the absolute ideal. His reflection is not that of an intellectual who delights in speculation: it is Christian doctrine directed toward practice.

As a moralist and a psychologist, this great pope does not address monks alone: he seeks to transform his doctrine and adapt it to all Christians, making it universal. His teachings unite all the aspects of morality and contemplation, as everything converges on the quest for virtuous action and contemplative prayer.[45]

For Gregory, the moral value of external acts is determined by the intention that precedes them. Setting the intention as the foundation of the moral value of every act means attributing fundamental importance to the examination and formation of this upright intention, which is achieved only after having applied discernment to separate good thoughts from evil ones. In his concern for the purity

---

43. Letter 213: *Letters*, III, p. 302 (*Lettere*, III, p. 236).
44. On Saint Gregory the Great (circa 540–604), see R. A. Markus, *Gregory the Great and His World*, Cambridge, 1997; J. Moorhead, *Gregory the Great*, London and New York, 2005.
45. See F. Dingjan, *Discretio*, op. cit., p. 87.

THE TRADITION OF *DISCRETIO*

of intention, Gregory insists on the importance of discretion understood as discernment, which is to say as a judgment capable of distinguishing between, and keeping watch over, one's thoughts.

In the *Morals on the Book of Job*, Gregory compares the many
thoughts that crowd the soul to a great multitude of servants who,
when the master of the home is gone, do not do their jobs and live in
confusion and disarray. Thoughts should therefore remain under the
authority of reason and should not dominate the soul by their multitude, treading on the sovereignty of our discretion (*ordine discretionis*) with their disarray. They should be governed by discreet reason
(*rationis discretione*).[46]

According to Saint Gregory, all of the inner movements of the
soul should be watched over with close attention before thoughts
turn into actions. This vigilance of the spirit, which separates virtues from vices, should not be lacking; otherwise, the door is open
to evil spirits seeking to destroy the soul.[47] Yet, even when temptation seems to have the upper hand on virtue, discretion survives as a
judgment of the conscience, as discernment, and is still able to carry
out its task of watching over thoughts, distinguishing good ones
from evil ones, and measuring the harm caused by temptation. For
example, in many passages from the second book of *Morals*, Gregory
reaffirms that "*rationis discretio*," "*discretio ratio mentis*," or "*mentis
discretio*" never succumbs despite the harms caused to the soul by
temptation: it always returns and shows the soul what it has lost.[48]
At times, in fact, thanks to temptation, discretion makes progress by
learning to distinguish better between virtues and vices.[49]

For Gregory, however, discretion is not limited to accurate discernment: it is also necessary for the upright fulfillment of the good

---

46. S. Gregory the Great, *Morals on the Book of Job*, 3 vols., Oxford, 1844–50, vol.
1, book i, xxx, para. 42, p. 55.

47. Ibid., vol. 1, book i, xxxv, para. 49, pp. 59–60.

48. Ibid., vol. 1, book ii, xlvi, para. 73, pp. 114–15; xlvii, para. 74, pp. 115–16; xlvii,
para. 75, pp. 116–18; xlix, para. 79, pp. 121–23.

49. Ibid., vol. 1, book ii, l, para. 80, p. 123.

intention by conferring the proper measure to the act. In all actions, one must behave with subtle discretion (*discretionis subtilitate*) to avoid excesses:[50] discretion enables the discernment not only of the action but also of proper measure in the action. In homily IX, for example, Saint Gregory specifies how to exercise authority with discretion by using proper measure, without excessive rigor yet without falling into weakness by mercy. In fact, readily granted forgiveness can further drive the culprit toward evil, and, conversely, excessive severity can worsen the harm to someone trying to mend his ways.[51]

Though Gregory is addressing all Christians, particularly in *Morals*, his teachings are first of all directed to the shepherds or pastors of souls. His *Pastoral Rule* is an unparalleled example of his attention to them, of his wisdom-filled spirit, and of moderation and understanding of the human heart, which are indispensable conditions for action suited to pastoral needs. Thus, Saint Gregory shows great psychological depth in chapter 36 of the *Pastoral Rule* by addressing thoughtfully the many pastoral needs.[52]

According to Gregory, the task of discretion is not to discern the origin of thoughts (*discretio spirituum* is absent from his teachings), but rather to distinguish good thoughts from evil ones and constantly keep watch. Even after the damage caused by temptation, the *rationis discretio* never succumbs and shows the soul what it has lost. In this sense, discretion is a judgment of the conscience or a form of discernment. In action, the function of discretion is to keep watch over the purity of the intentions and their actual fulfillment with proper measure.[53]

Several clear points of resemblance emerge when comparing Gregory's and Catherine's discretion. In addition to the image of the

50. Ibid., vol. 3, book xxviii, xi, para. 26, pp. 282–83.
51. Gregory the Great, *Homilies on the Book of the Prophet Ezekiel* (2nd edn., T. Tomkinson, tr.), Etna, CA, 2008, book ii, homily ix, para. 18.
52. Gregory the Great, *The Book of Pastoral Rule* (G. E. Demacopoulos, tr.), Crestwood, NY, 2007, part iii, ch. 36, pp. 202–3.
53. See F. Dingjan, *Discretio*, op. cit., pp. 101–2.

light of discretion (*lumen discretionis*),[54] which Gregory uses occasionally and very often recurs in Catherine, there are similarities in at least two other respects. The first is the importance Gregory attributes to inner reflection, which is to say the discernment to distinguish between good and evil thoughts. The second is the vigilance of discretion in the fulfillment of the act, to be carried out with proper measure. In relation to the first point, it has repeatedly been noted how Catherine emphasizes true knowledge, which is the fundamental requirement for discretion and can only be attained within the cell of one's inner life. In relation to the second point, suffice it to recall the importance she attributes to the duty of rendering the debt in the concrete fulfillment of what knowledge has shown and taught.

5. SAINT BERNARD

Saint Bernard[55] has been seen as the symbol of the whole spiritual literature that is an extension of the Patristic age. Following the tradition of the Church Fathers, he expresses himself with images and comparisons taken from the Bible and a poetic vocabulary, similar to biblical vocabulary, which does not prevent him from engaging in theological reflection. The same can be said of his thinking on discretion: while lacking precise philosophical notions, the many passages on discretion in Bernard's works efficaciously condense the best of what earlier authors had written on it.

---

54. Gregory the Great, *The Book of Pastoral Rule*, op. cit., part iii, ch. 35, p. 201 ("light of discernment"). See also S. Gregory the Great, *Morals on the Book of Job*, op. cit., vol. 3, book xxviii, xi, para. 30, pp. 285–86.

55. On Saint Bernard (1090 or 1091–1153), see T. Merton, *The Last of the Fathers. Saint Bernard of Clairvaux and the Encyclical Letter Doctor Mellifluus*, New York, 1954; G. R. Evans, *Bernard of Clairvaux*, New York and Oxford, 2000. On Bernard's spirituality, see J. R. Sommerfeldt, *The Spiritual Teachings of Bernard of Clairvaux: An Intellectual History of the Early Cistercian Order*, Kalamazoo, MI, 1991.

For example, in sermon 49, discretion has the role of regulating every virtue, and this order "assigns proportion and beauty, and even permanence."[56] Discretion even gives order to charity, as it is all the more necessary where there is greater passion. In sermon 23, Bernard affirms that, without the fervor of charity, "the virtue of discretion is lifeless" and, conversely, "intense fervor goes headlong without the curb of discretion": for this reason, one who possesses both, namely "the fervor that enlivens discretion, the discretion that regulates fervor," is praiseworthy.[57]

Even when charity is sincere, the guidance of discretion is indispensable to find the most suitable means and the proper measure for expressing charity. Only God can enlighten the darkness of man so that man can see in himself "an ordered charity which knows and loves only what is worthy of love and in the measure that it is worthy of love and for the reasons that it is worthy of love."[58] This enlightenment is the light of discretion, which is "the mother of virtues and the sum of perfection. The teaching of discretion is, 'Avoid extremes.'"[59]

In sermon 49, Saint Bernard points out that discretion "is not so much a virtue as a moderator and guide of the virtues, a director of the affections, a teacher of right living."[60] This affirmation does not appear to conflict with the earlier traditional doctrine that, in reality, had never pronounced on the value of discretion as a virtue, but rather on its relationship to the other virtues. In harmony with this tradition, though still without precise philosophical notions, Bernard limits himself to saying that discretion is more the coordinating,

56. Bernard of Clairvaux, *On the Song of Songs* (K. Walsh and I. M. Edmonds, tr.), vol. 3, Kalamazoo, MI, 1979, II.5, p. 25.

57. Ibid. (K. Walsh tr.), vol. 2, Kalamazoo, MI, 1976, III.8, p. 32.

58. Bernard of Clairvaux, *The Letters* (B. S. James, tr.), Chicago, 1953, letter 87 (letter 85 in the traditional numbering), pp. 124–27, at para. 3, p. 126.

59. Bernard of Clairvaux, *Sermons for Advent and the Christmas Season* (J. Leinenweber, ed., I. Edmonds, W. M. Beckett, and C. Greenia, tr.), Kalamazoo, MI, 2007, "On the Lord's Circumcision, Sermon Three (On Spiritual Circumcision)," pp. 144–53, at p. 152, para. 11.

60. Bernard of Clairvaux, *On the Song of Songs*, vol. 3, op. cit., II.5, p. 25.

guiding, and moderating principle of virtues than (and this is not a total negation) a virtue in itself.

Evident similarities emerge when comparing Bernard's with Catherine's discretion. First of all, Bernard's reference to the light of discretion is a familiar image in Catherine. Furthermore, according to Saint Bernard, discretion guides the fervor of charity, and this calls to mind what Catherine affirms with regard to charity, which should be ordered by discretion because it would otherwise be indiscreet: discretion, which is "born of charity" and sets no limit to love of God, gives order to love of neighbor.[61]

Last, Bernard attributes importance to the knowledge of oneself, which he considers to be the starting point for attaining the knowledge of God. According to him, the knowledge of oneself is a necessary component of the spiritual searching by all beginners and the primary task of novices. Knowledge of self is found not only at the beginning of one's spiritual life in the search for God but also at its end: knowing oneself means discovering the divine image—and therefore the presence of God—in oneself.[62] Its condition is humility: the soul attains knowledge of its wretchedness and its beauty through humility, and this twofold knowledge provides clarity for action. Likewise, in Catherine, the knowledge of oneself and of God, as the spiritual basis and the fundamental requirement for discretion, is closely linked to humility, which is the evidence proving that man has achieved true knowledge. As was mentioned before, in letter 197, Catherine ends up equating the two notions by referring to "humility or true self-knowledge."[63]

---

61. *Dialogue*, p. 44, ch. 11 (*Dialogo*, pp. 34–35).

62. É. Gilson has written that, for Saint Bernard, "the man who seeks to know himself acknowledges at one time his misery and his greatness: his misery in that he is nothing in himself; his greatness in that he is made in God's image by freedom" (*La Théologie mystique de saint Bernard* (4th edn.), Paris 1980, p. 221).

63. *Letters*, II, p. 428 (*Lettere*, III, p. 165).

6. RICHARD OF SAINT VICTOR

Discretion holds an important place in the spirituality of Richard of Saint Victor.[64] Although the great Victorine theologian does not appear to adhere to a rigorous philosophical system, his doctrine on discretion, as it emerges from various passages of his works, reveals considerable and consistent reflection on the topic.

According to Richard, since the ultimate end of man is contemplating God, to reach this elevated end, it is first necessary to prepare the cognitive and affective faculties for an ever greater knowledge of the sensible world, of the soul (*cognitio sui*), and of God. This knowledge cannot be acquired without the purification of one's faculties by means of exercising the virtues.

Discretion is key to this ascesis, which the author describes through efficacious biblical symbolism in *Benjamin Minor*, representing the role that knowledge should have to allow order and measure to reign in all moral living. In chapter 67, through an allegorical exegesis of the passage in *Genesis* regarding Jacob and his children, Richard defines *discretion* as the virtue without which "nothing is sought for, nothing completed, nothing preserved."[65] It is acquired through great experience and only after having exercised the other virtues, because it is only after the extensive practice necessary for disciplining one's virtues that a perfect discernment of one's behavior can be achieved.[66] Indeed, the discernment of what should be done in the countless concrete cases is acquired only after having exerted many great efforts in the practice of each virtue. In so doing, while it is inevitable that man often falls, it is necessary that he get

---

64. On Richard of Saint Victor (?–1173) and his spirituality, see M. Lenglart, *La théorie de la contemplation dans l'œuvre de Richard de Saint-Victor*, Paris, 1935.

65. Richard of St. Victor, *The Twelve Patriarchs; The Mystical Ark; Book Three of the Trinity* (G. A. Zinn, tr.), New York, 1979, p. 124, ch. lxvii.

66. "If one wants to acquire the virtues, it is necessary to know not only how one must be but also how one is; one cannot govern what one does not know" (F. Dingjan, *Discretio*, op. cit., p. 174).

back up "and through frequent falling learn what vigilance, what caution is necessary to acquire and keep the good things of virtue."[67] At the end of the same chapter, Richard clarifies that, since only reason can discern and carry out an act of intelligence, there can be no doubt that "discretion is born from reason alone."[68]

Richard also affirms in *Benjamin Minor* that both the grace of discretion[69] and the grace of contemplation derive from reason, and, in this work, they are symbolized by Joseph and Benjamin, respectively. According to the author, it is first necessary to know oneself to attain knowledge of God: man must "first learn to know his own invisible things before he presumes that he is able to grasp at invisible divine things."[70] Richard then reaffirms the importance of knowledge of self for attaining knowledge of God in chapter 78. Using the image of the mountain on the peak of which Christ was transfigured, Richard asks: "Do you wish to hear the mystery of the Father's secrets? Ascend this mountain; learn to know yourself."[71] This is because it is in oneself that the rational soul finds "that it is the foremost and principal mirror for seeing God."[72]

In Richard's reflection, discretion therefore comes to take on a fundamental and irreplaceable role: it is rational knowledge of oneself that can only be acquired through the purification of one's faculties by means of exercising the virtues. In fact, according to him, virtue should be ordered and measured: it is ordered when it tends to that toward which it should tend, and measured when it is as great and strong as it should be. With these two terms, *ordinatus* and

---

67. Richard of St. Victor, *The Twelve Patriarchs*, op. cit., p. 124, ch. lxvii.

68. Ibid., p. 125, ch. lxvii.

69. In another writing, Richard notes that one attains the grace of discretion through a great experience of the virtues and, above all, of the teachings of revealing grace (*Sermons et opuscules spirituels inédits* (J. Chatillon et al., eds.), Paris, 1951, vol. 1, pp. 32–33 ("L'édit d'Alexandre ou Les trois processions")).

70. Richard of St. Victor, *The Twelve Patriarchs*, op. cit., p. 129, ch. lxxi.

71. Ibid., p. 136, ch. lxxviii.

72. Ibid., p. 129, ch. lxxii.

moderatus, the author indicates the two functions of discretion: distinguishing good from evil and the proper measure in achieving the end.

According to the Victorine, it is therefore necessary that everyone carefully control his own "affections" so they are not only ordered but also moderate. Indeed, excessive fear becomes desperation, overly intense sorrow becomes bitterness, hope without measure becomes presumption, exaggerated love becomes adulation, pointless joy becomes dissipation, and uncontrolled anger becomes rage. Virtues "are turned into vices if they are not moderated by discretion."[73] For this reason, discretion must follow after all the other virtues, as it must judge them all: except by discretion, "the soul neither comprehends nor corrects the hurtful deeds of the virtues."[74]

Richard distinguishes five acts within discretion: (1) *diiudicatio* is the upright judgment that gives the virtues direction toward their ends, since it is the light that leads toward truth (*"lucerna cordis iudicium discretionis"*); (2) *deliberatio* makes the distinction between what should and should not be done in a concrete case, taking into account the particular circumstances; (3) *dispositio* establishes order among the means that are helpful for attaining the end; (4) *dispensatio* distinguishes between what is appropriate and inappropriate and reexamines the first judgment when the circumstances require it; and (5) *moderatio* determines the measure and moderation of the action, because a licit, helpful action determined for the right moment in accordance with the demands of the situation might lose its goodness if not carried out in proper measure. Discretion comprises all these acts, including their concrete fulfillment, because the good intention of the conscience and deliberation are not sufficient (and therefore not virtuous): they must be put into practice.

Richard further distinguishes between three degrees of discretion corresponding to the three age groups: while the beginnings

73. Ibid., p. 123, ch. lxvi.
74. Ibid., p. 126, ch. lxviii.

of discretion and strength are found in children and can increase in adolescents, it is only in adulthood that they can reach perfection[75] because the perfection of discretion can only be the fruit of experience and of the constant and ongoing practice of all virtues.

In Richard, therefore, discretion holds an extremely important role in the moral and spiritual life: it is discretion that discerns and judges, orders and moderates, and because of this function is found within all virtues. Discretion is also at the center of the relationship between charity and knowledge: perfect charity and true discretion are so inseparable that having the one implies having the other. The role of discretion also applies to the mystical impulse: it must defend against irrationality and unrestraint, ensuring that what is loved is worthy of being loved and establishing a hierarchy between what is loved and the proper measure of that love.[76]

This reflection on the relationship between charity and discretion extends to the Trinity. In the treatise *De Trinitate*, the idea of *caritas ordinata* allows Richard to affirm that divine charity demands a plurality of divine Persons and their equality. In the third book of this work, after having identified the altruism of charity in God,[77] Richard tries to show that, if one seeks to maintain rigorous proportionality of dignity between supreme charity and its object, it is necessary to accept the plurality of divine Persons, their sovereign equality, and their sovereign similitude. In the seventh chapter of the same book, *caritas ordinata* is called "*amor discretus*": it is love accompanied by discretion, which requires that the object of sovereign charity be likewise sovereignly lovable in God. Thus, he who must be sovereignly loved in accordance with all the opulence of sovereign charity must undoubtedly be worthy to be sovereignly loved in accordance with

---

75. Richard de Saint-Victor, *Sermons*, op. cit., pp. 74–75 ("Les trois processions").

76. See G. Dumeige, *Richard de Saint-Victor et l'idée chrétienne de l'amour*, Paris, 1962, pp. 65–66.

77. On this, F. Guimet has observed that Richard is at the confluence of two traditions: one inherited from Gregory the Great and the other from Origen ("*Caritas ordinata* et *amor discretus* dans la théologie trinitaire de Richard de Saint-Victor," in *Revue du moyen âge latin* 4 (1948), pp. 225–36, at p. 225).

the supreme law of discretion.[78] At the end of the same chapter, the author concludes by affirming that, just as the nature of charity demands plurality of Persons in true divinity, likewise the perfection of this charity requires supreme equality of Persons in actual plurality. Total equality requires total similitude because it is possible to have similitude without equality but never equality without reciprocal similitude.[79]

Richard then uses this doctrine of rigorous proportionality between supreme charity and its object to demonstrate that *caritas ordinata* is equivalent to *amor discretus*, which is to say the perfect equality of knowing and loving in God. At the same time, this trinitarian speculation reveals the importance of discretion in Richard's spiritual teaching: in man, it is called to regulate the whole moral life by giving preeminence to order and measure, through a variety of functions that extend primarily to the virtues. In God, however, who does not need to exercise this variety of functions, discretion is limited to ensuring correspondence between sovereign charity and the sovereign lovability of its object.

Comparing Richard's to Catherine's discretion, there is clearly great affinity between these two spiritual authors regarding the close relationship between discretion and knowledge of oneself. Richard entrusts discretion with a fundamental role in the spiritual life, above all in terms of knowledge of the sensible world and of the soul. Man can acquire this knowledge only through the purification of his

78. This is what Richard of Saint Victor writes in book 3 of his treatise on the Trinity: "But love is not discerning where one is loved supremely who should not be loved supremely. But in supremely wise goodness, just as the flame of love does not burn otherwise than supreme wisdom prescribes, so it also does not burn more intensely. And so it is necessary that one who should be loved supremely according to that supreme abundance of charity without doubt should love according to that supreme rule of discretion" (*The Twelve Patriarchs*, op. cit., pp. 379–80, ch. vii).

79. "And so in true Divinity, as the particular nature of charity requires a plurality of persons, so the integrity of the same charity requires supreme equality of persons in true plurality. However, so that the persons may be equal in everything, it is necessary that they be similar in everything. For similitude can be possessed without equality, while equality is never possessed without mutual similitude" (ibid., p. 380, ch. vii).

own faculties and through the exercise of the virtues: it is only after many efforts in the practice of each virtue that man can attain that discernment that is necessary to determine what should be done in concrete cases. Furthermore, according to the Victorine, knowledge of oneself is necessary for attaining knowledge of God: it is in itself that the rational soul finds the mirror for seeing God.[80]

Likewise, in Catherine's writings, there is great emphasis on the knowledge of self and of God. This is at the root of her entire spirituality and is the indispensable requirement for discretion. It is within this context that she uses the image of the soul as a mirror, in which we see ourselves in God, as his creatures, and God in us, by virtue of the union God brought about between his divinity and our humanity.[81]

Another element of similarity between the two authors has to do with discretion considered in its concrete fulfillment. For Richard, discretion is a form of knowledge that must be extended to the whole moral life to uphold order and measure. This element is also present in Catherine, in the form of rendering the debt (as was amply discussed earlier in this study).

Yet another point of analogy is the role of discretion in relation to charity. According to Richard, discretion regulates charity, and not only in human beings. His trinitarian speculation leads him to affirm the equivalence between *caritas ordinata* and *amor discretus*, between knowledge and love in God. For him, while discretion in human beings has the task of regulating the whole moral life, in God it ensures correspondence between sovereign charity and the sovereign lovability of its object. For Catherine, too, charity must be ordered by discretion. She recognizes an order within charity according to which one must set neither law nor limit in loving God, whereas one must love one's neighbor with ordered charity. This means that material goods may be sacrificed for the others, and even one's own life may be

---

80. Richard seems to have borrowed this theme of the mirror from Saint Anselm, who had shown, in his *Monologium*, that knowledge of self inevitably moves toward knowledge of God. The soul is like a mirror in which to contemplate the divine image.

81. *Dialogue*, pp. 365–66, ch. 167 (*Dialogo*, p. 586).

sacrificed for the spiritual good of one's neighbor, but one's spiritual good cannot be sacrificed because it would involve an offense against God: "a well-ordered love in God is unwilling to give up our soul even to save the whole world. Even if it were possible to send everyone to eternal life by committing a single sin, we must not do it."[82]

Finally, Catherine and Richard are somewhat close in applying discretion to divine charity. In the *Dialogue*, one reads that God gave humanity his only-begotten Son, thus providing for man's need "with great prudence," in the sense that God caught the devil with the "bait" of humanity and the "hook" of divinity.[83] It must be admitted, though, that the similarities between the two authors on this last point remain vague, because Richard's trinitarian reflection on *caritas ordinata* or *amor discretus* is absent from Catherine.

7. CONCLUSION

Richard of Saint Victor is the last author in the Christian tradition to have dealt with *discretio* in such an extensive manner. It is also with the great Victorine that this brief survey draws to a close, having examined just a few of the more significant authors among those who have addressed the topic of *discretio*. Their reflections, while lacking precise philosophical or theological categories, are profound and articulate. From this body of teachings, which was developed primarily in the monastic context with the aim of indicating the path to achieve perfection and contemplation, one can draw an understanding of discretion that includes not only the discernment of good and evil thoughts or good and evil intentions but also their upright fulfillment in moral and spiritual action. This notion would later be inherited by Scholasticism, leading to Aquinas's synthesis on the virtue of prudence as its point of culmination.

82. *Letters*, II, p. 296 (*Lettere*, IV, p. 81).
83. *Dialogue*, p. 278, ch. 135 (*Dialogo*, p. 431).

From Augustine to Aquinas's Synthesis of the Tradition of *Discretio* with the Aristotelian Teaching on Prudence

1. INTRODUCTION

As in Catherine *discretion* and *prudence* are synonyms, comparing Catherine's notion of discretion with the preceding tradition requires also the treatment, however brief, of prudence. The concept of prudence in Greek and Roman philosophy (mainly Platonism and Stoicism) considerably influenced the Church Fathers by way of Cicero's mediation.[1]

The introduction of the qualifying adjective *cardinal* in reference to the four moral virtues of prudence, justice, fortitude, and temperance was due to Saint Ambrose.[2] Though inspired by Cicero's *De Officiis*, the bishop of Milan presents the virtue of prudence in decidedly Christian terms, with examples from the Bible and the history of salvation. Ambrose insists on the intellectual aspect of prudence

---

1. D. Tettamanzi, *Verità e fede—Temi e prospettive di morale cristiana*, Casale Monferrato, 1993, p. 330.
2. On Saint Ambrose (circa 340–397), see A. Paredi, *Saint Ambrose, His Life and Times* (M. J. Costelloe, tr.), Notre Dame, IN, 1964; N. B. McLynn, *Ambrose of Milan: Church and Court in a Christian Capital*, Berkeley, CA, 1994.

COMPARISON IN HISTORICAL PERSPECTIVE

and its relationship to the other virtues and to the truth. Prudence has the primary task of allowing man to distinguish between what is divine and what is human, leading man to renounce the goods of this world to seek God.

The moral notion of *discretio*, in Ambrose's reflection, essentially corresponds to that of prudence, and this is also true of Saint Augustine.

2. SAINT AUGUSTINE

Augustine[3] refers more to prudence, understood as the art of living well and attaining eternal happiness, than to *discretio*. This great theologian outlines the various aspects of prudence, such as vigilant attention to avoid danger and discernment between good and evil.[4] In particular, Augustine stresses the link between the various other virtues and charity, configuring prudence as mediation and a form of love. One of his better known passages addresses precisely this point:

> As to virtue leading us to a happy life, I hold virtue to be nothing else than perfect love of God. For the fourfold division of virtue I regard as taken from four forms of love. For these four virtues (would that all felt their influence in their minds as they have their names in their mouths!), I should have no hesitation in defining them: that temperance is love giving itself entirely to that which is loved; fortitude is love readily bearing all things for the sake of the loved object; justice is love serving only the loved object, and therefore ruling rightly; prudence is love distinguishing with sagacity between what hinders it and what helps it. The

---

3. On Saint Augustine (354–430), see the classic biography by P. Brown, *Augustine of Hippo: A Biography* (new edn.), Berkeley, CA, 2000. For an introduction to Augustine's thought, see H. Chadwick, *Augustine: A Very Short Introduction*, Oxford, 2001.
    4. See D. Tettamanzi, *Verità e fede*, op. cit., pp. 335–36.

object of this love is not anything, but only God, the chief good, the highest wisdom, the perfect harmony. So we may express the definition thus: that temperance is love keeping itself entire and incorrupt for God; fortitude is love bearing everything readily for the sake of God; justice is love serving God only, and therefore ruling well all else, as subject to man; prudence is love making a right distinction between what helps it towards God and what might hinder it.[5]

Recalling the divine origin of virtues, in his battle against the Pelagian controversy, Augustine affirms that prudence, on account of which we distinguish between good and evil, is one of the four virtues we need to practice in our lives. From these virtues, in this life, we will progress to a single virtue, the "virtue of contemplating God alone." In that life, "prudence will not be necessary," because we will not encounter any evils we need to avoid.[6]

One of the most important aspects in Augustine is knowledge of self. In the years leading up to his conversion, and those shortly after that, the underlying motif of Augustine's meditation was the relationship between the soul and God. These two spiritual realities were the focus of his philosophical and theological reflection, which were in turn based on the metaphysics of the inner life. From the proofs of the existence of the soul to the demonstration of the existence of God, the life-giving principle that drives Augustine's intellectual search is the principle of the inner life, clearly formulated in

5. Augustine, "On the Morals of the Catholic Church" ("*De Moribus Ecclesiae Catholicae*," R. Stothert, tr.), in *Nicene and Post-Nicene Fathers*, First Series, vol. 4 ("Augustin: The Writings against the Manichaens, and against the Donatists," P. Schaff, ed.), Peabody, MA, 1994 (originally published 1887), pp. 41–63, at p. 48, ch. 15, para. 25. (In footnote 7 on the same page, at the end of the passage that has been quoted, A. H. Newman remarked: "It would be difficult to find in Christian literature a more beautiful and satisfactory exposition of the love of God. The Neo-Platonic influence is manifest, but it is Neo-Platonism thoroughly Christianized.")

6. Augustine, *Expositions of the Psalms 73–98* (J. E. Rotelle, ed., M. Boulding, tr.; Part III, vol. 18, of *The Works of Saint Augustine. A Translation for the 21st Century*), New York, 2002, p. 199, para. 11.

the concise expression "do not go out of yourself; enter into yourself" ("*redi in te ipsum*").[7] For Augustine, "entering into oneself" is the method of philosophical investigation aimed at discovering the truth. He shows his direct experience of this inner journey in the *Confessions*, where he writes:

> By the Platonic books I was admonished to return into myself.... With you as my guide I entered into my innermost citadel, and was given power to do so because you had become my helper (Ps. 29:11). I entered and with my soul's eye, such as it was, saw above that same eye of my soul the immutable light higher than my mind—not the light of every day, obvious to anyone, nor a larger version of the same kind which would, as it were, have given out a much brighter light and filled everything with its magnitude.... It was not that light, but a different thing, utterly different from all our kinds of light. It transcended my mind, not in the way that oil floats on water, nor as heaven is above earth. It was superior because it made me, and I was inferior because I was made by it. The person who knows the truth knows it, and he who knows it knows eternity.[8]

The road of the inner life, focused on a genuine itinerary of inner purification, is also an ascetic and experiential journey. It is only when one is immersed in the profound depths of one's own self that one can attain knowledge of self and, through this, knowledge of God. This concept is at the root of Augustine's famous passage in the *Confessions*:

---

7. Augustine, *Of True Religion* (J. H. S. Burleigh, tr.), Chicago, 1959, pp. 68–69, xxxix, para. 72. This theme, so crucial in Saint Augustine, had already been treated by Saint Ambrose, his teacher.

8. Augustine, *Confessions* (H. Chadwick, ed.), Oxford and New York, 1991, x (16), p. 123.

Late have I loved you, beauty so old and so new: late have I loved you. And see, you were within and I was in the external world and sought you there, and in my unlovely state I plunged into those lovely created things which you made.[9]

Augustine's *"reditus ad seipsum"* and the importance of the inner life in his thought show evident similarities with the inner cell in which Catherine invites all to dwell to achieve that twofold knowledge of oneself and God that is the fundamental requirement for discretion; however, entering into oneself does not certainly constitute for Catherine a method of philosophical study the way it does for Augustine.

Another element of similarity between the two saints has to do with the three faculties of the soul, which Augustine identifies as memory, intellect, and will.[10] For Catherine, the greatest gift God has given to the "creatures endowed with reason," other than their very being, is the ability to know the triune God. This is reflected in the three faculties of the human soul: memory, intellect, and will. They make it possible for man, created in the image and likeness of the triune God, to know and love him:

I provided you with the gift of memory so that you might hold fast my benefits and be made a sharer in my own, the eternal Father's power. I gave you understanding so that in the wisdom of my only-begotten Son you might comprehend and know what I the eternal Father want, I who gave you graces with such burning love. I gave you a will to love, making you a sharer in the Holy Spirit's mercy, so that you might love what your understanding sees and knows.[11]

9. Ibid., xxvii (38), p. 201.
10. See Augustine, *On the Trinity. Books 8–15* (G. B. Matthews, ed., S. McKenna, tr.), Cambridge, 2002, book xv, pp. 167–224.
11. *Dialogue*, p. 277, ch. 135 (*Dialogo*, pp. 429–30). On the similarities between Augustine and Catherine regarding the three faculties of the soul, B. Hackett has written: "The basis of her doctrine is Augustine's comparison of the soul with the Trinity,

There is therefore an obvious influence of Augustine on Catherine, even though scholars, in their majority, prefer to speak of an indirect contribution. The Augustinian William Flete, who was known in Catherine's circle as the "bachelor," supposedly influenced Catherine's thinking, but those who have studied this question in some detail tend to suggest that Flete's influence on Catherine is considerably less than once thought.[12]

As Catherine had no direct knowledge of Augustine's writings, and of the majority of spiritual writers who preceded her, she probably entered into contact with their ideas by listening to the

one of his most acute and penetrating analyses of the soul in its threefold constitution, and described by him in masterly and unique skill in *The Trinity*. Nevertheless, he would not go the whole way with Catherine in identifying the memory with the power of the Father, the intellect with the wisdom of the Son, and the will with the love or, as Catherine most often calls it, the clemency of the Holy Spirit, but he does make the suggestion" (*William Flete, O.S.A., and Catherine of Siena*, op. cit., p. 115). In reality, Catherine does not identify the three faculties with the Trinity, but speaks of "participation" in letter 286: "Being so sweetly raised into the midst of the Trinity, [participating] as I've said in the Father's power, the Son's wisdom, and the Holy Spirit's mercy" (*Letters*, III, p. 54; *Lettere*, IV, p. 210).

12. The question of the influence of Augustine's doctrine on Catherine is complex. See (with a critical eye), B. Hackett, *William Flete, O.S.A., and Catherine of Siena*, op. cit., at pp. 107–15; B. Hackett, "The Augustinian Tradition in the Mysticism of St. Catherine of Siena," in F. van Fleteren, J. C. Schnaubelt and J. Reino (eds.), *Augustine Mystic and Mystagogue*, New York, 1994, pp. 493–512. In R. Fawtier and L. Canet, *La double expérience*, op. cit., p. 247, Canet wrote that Catherine depends on Augustine rather than Thomas. This and other statements in that work, though, have rightly been criticized in I. Taurisano, "La vera Caterina da Siena e l'ultima opera di R. Fawtier," in *Vita Cristiana* 18 (1949), pp. 223–34; E. Dupré Theseider, "La duplice esperienza di S. Caterina," in *Rivista Storica Italiana* 62 (1950), pp. 533–74. In turn, according to A. Grion, the greatest influence on Catherine was that of William Flete, who would have brought to Catherine's knowledge what Grion regards as "the source of the sources" of her thought, namely the *Arbor vitae crucifixae Jesu* by Ubertino da Casale (*Santa Caterina da Siena. Dottrina e fonti*, Brescia, 1953, pp. 275–85). This alleged Augustinian influence, however, has appropriately been reduced to its true weight by G. D'Urso, who has also shown how grossly exaggerated is the presumed impact on Catherine by Ubertino da Casale ("Il pensiero di S. Caterina e le sue fonti," in *Sapienza* 7 (1954), pp. 335–88, an article that was later revised and published in *Urbis et orbis*, op. cit., pp. 218–73).

preachers.[13] According to Dupré Theseider, many times "Catherine re-echoes, often by memory, the 'authoritative sources' of which she had indirect knowledge and which were the common heritage of writers and preachers of the time."[14]

Other than through *The Mirror of the Cross* by Domenico Cavalca,[15] it is therefore highly probable that many of Augustine's ideas reached Catherine through the filter of preachers, particularly Dominicans.[16] The fact remains, though, that, despite Augustine's indirect contribution to the spiritual treasure of ideas and images used by Catherine, nothing warrants the conclusion that Catherine may have had an Augustinian formation.

As to the tradition of prudence, apart from Augustine's contribution, there was no systematic treatment during the Patristic age. There was not even a unanimous definition of this virtue, which was generally considered only in close connection with the three other cardinal virtues. It was primarily *discretio* that was studied and

13. G. Cavallini has rightly noted that the problem of Catherine's sources remains open and that Augustine's and Thomas's influence was probably filtered by preachers (*S. Domenico e i suoi frati nella spiritualità di S. Caterina da Siena*, Napoli and Bari, 1993, p. 60).

14. *Epistolario di Santa Caterina da Siena* (E. Dupré Theseider, ed.), op. cit., p. lxxxix.

15. This work is discussed later. According to the authoritative T. S. Centi (in his article "Il pensiero di Agostino negli scritti di S. Caterina da Siena," in *Augustinus et Thomas* 34 (1986), pp. 380–92), Catherine's knowledge of Augustine was indirect, as the writings of the saints, during her time, were not available in the vernacular. What reached a wide audience was instead the work of two Dominican friars, namely Domenico Cavalca (*The Mirror of the Cross*) and Jacopo Passavanti (*The Mirror of True Penance*). These two writings contained ample quotations from the works of the Church Fathers. T. S. Centi suggests that it is sufficient to compare *The Mirror of the Cross* with Catherine's writings to realize how Catherine may have used some of Augustine's passages as reported by Cavalca.

16. In addition to Cavalca and Passavanti, another Dominican friar whose writings (starting from the influential *Legenda aurea*) were a source of inspiration to preachers at the time of Catherine is blessed Giacomo (or Iacopo) da Varazze. G. D'Urso has recalled how the Augustinian "*noverim te, noverim me*," a constant theme in Giacomo da Varazze, would prompt in Catherine her own personal reflection on the double knowledge of self and God ("Giacomo da Varazze, maestro di S. Caterina da Siena," in *Quaderni Cateriniani* 47–48 (1989), pp. 1–17).

recommended, though prudence was at times presented in combination with it. For example, a discussion of the four moral virtues is almost entirely lacking in Cassian, who essentially identifies prudence with *discretio*. The same combination of the two notions is also found in other spiritual writers, such as Benedict and Richard of Saint Victor.[17]

The first theologian who made an effort to group the various aspects of prudence into a coherent body of doctrine, around the year 1220, was William of Auxerre. Yet it was only when the complete Latin translation of Aristotle's *Nicomachean Ethics* (the most comprehensive work of ethics of antiquity, with an entire book on prudence) became available that a more thorough study of the first cardinal virtue began. It was conducted by Albert the Great, whose oral teachings were collected and edited by Thomas Aquinas. It would be this great theologian who would first explicitly identify discretion with prudence by merging the tradition of *discretio* with the Aristotelian teaching on prudence.

3. SAINT THOMAS AQUINAS

For Thomas Aquinas,[18] the reflection on Aristotelian philosophy became a component, along with the study of the biblical text and the data from the Patristic tradition, of a theological synthesis carrying the marks of true science.

Aquinas often refers to *discretio* in his works, showing his familiarity with the earlier tradition. In Aquinas's passages on *discretio*, all

17. Until the thirteenth century the reference was to discretion, not prudence, even though in Cassian, Benedict, and Richard of Saint Victor, the two notions were close to one another.

18. Obviously, the bibliography on the life and works of Thomas Aquinas (1224/5–1274) is too vast to attempt here any selection. It is therefore sufficient to refer to the two introductory works by J.-P. Torrell, *Saint Thomas Aquinas. Volume 1: The Person and His Work* (revised edn., R. Royal, tr.), Washington, DC, 2005; and *Saint Thomas Aquinas. Volume 2: Spiritual Master* (R. Royal, tr.), Washington, DC, 2003.

the characteristic features that tradition had assigned to this virtue are attributed to *discretio* as an act of prudence.[19] In his treatise on the virtue of prudence, in questions 47 to 56 of the II-II of the *Summa Theologica*,[20] Aquinas identifies *discretio* with prudence.

In his systematic presentation of moral teaching, Thomas Aquinas places on purpose his exposition on prudence after the threefold treatise on the theological virtues. In fact, if the three theological virtues (faith, hope, and charity) are the principles of the supernatural moral life, the virtue of prudence is indispensable for applying these principles to the practical guidance of a virtuous life and for carrying out moral actions. Prudential reason presupposes a form of spirituality based on love of the good and a firm will to attain it; it presupposes that man believes, hopes, and loves God.

It is only through divine grace that human beings are freely elevated by God to the supernatural level receiving faith, hope, and love. Through faith, they come to know their supernatural end, which is God, because faith is the assent of the intellect to divine revelation. Through hope, human beings hope to reach their beatitude in God. Through charity, they love God as the natural and supernatural end of their lives.[21]

To have the ability to carry out, in practice, moral actions by living in conformity with God's will, and testing his faith, hope, and

19. See S. Thomae Aquinatis, *Scriptum super Sententiis magistri Petri Lombardi* (M. F. Moos, ed.), Parisiis, 1933, tomus III, p. 1057, para. 200 (lib. iii sententiarum, d. 33, q. 2, a. 3).

20. Thomas had already delineated the role of prudence vis-à-vis the other moral virtues earlier in the *Summa Theologica*, in the part dedicated to the moral act in general (I-II, q. 56, a. 3; qq. 57, 58, and 61).

21. Having demonstrated the primacy of the final cause on all other causes, Thomas shows that the human creature, which is capable of knowing and loving God, wills all that it wills in view of its final end. In this respect, Aquinas distinguishes between a natural and a supernatural final end (the beatitude in God), to which the natural one is subordinated. The will tends to the universal good like the intellect tends to the universal truth. The universal good cannot be anything created, which is good only by participation, but can only be God, who is also the universal truth (I-II, qq. 1-3).

charity, man has to receive more than just the theological virtues: he also needs the infused or supernatural moral virtues, which are the necessary extension of charity. Aquinas distinguishes between two orders of moral virtues: natural or acquired virtues, which are proportionate to the natural end of man (his knowledge, desires, and possibilities), and supernatural or infused virtues, which are linked to the existence of the supernatural end and are not proportionate to any acquired habit or natural moral virtue.[22] The Angelic Doctor writes:

> There are some dispositions whereby a man is directed to a goal which exceeds human powers.... Now dispositions must correspond to the goal to which they dispose; so dispositions which direct to a superhuman goal must themselves exceed the power of human nature. It follows that such dispositions could never be possessed by men unless infused by God: as is the case with all virtues which are due to grace.[23]

Special divine intervention as to the actions regarding intermediate ends is therefore necessary to make them intrinsically proportionate to the ultimate supernatural end and to the theological virtues. This infusion of supernatural moral virtues does not detract from, but rather demands, the presence of corresponding moral virtues in

22. See I–II, q. 63, aa. 3 and 4; q. 65, aa. 2 and 3. Aquinas distinguishes between acquired prudence, which is acquired by the repetition of the acts, and supernatural prudence, which is divinely infused. It is the latter that regulates moral life. In II–II, q. 47, a. 13, Aquinas also distinguishes among false prudence (aimed at an evil end), true prudence (aimed at a good end but not yet at the universal end of the whole life), and true and perfect prudence (which deliberates, judges, and orders everything to the end of the whole life).

23. St. Thomas Aquinas, *Summa Theologiae*, vol. 22 ("Dispositions for human acts" (1a2ae, 49–54), A. Kenny, tr.), London and New York, 1964, I–II, q. 51, a. 4, p. 65. The notion of "disposition" or "habit," derived from Aristotle, holds a central place in Aquinas's moral theology. The phases of man's human development are correlative to the establishment and growth of his habits, namely, those connatural dispositions through which man can easily carry out his acts.

accordance with the principle that the natural is the substantial cognitive and operative foundation of the supernatural.

Having thus centered morality on God as the final end of human life and having stressed that the theological and moral virtues are necessary to attain this end, Aquinas defines prudence as an "essentially intellectual" virtue. But he adds that prudence, while essentially an intellectual virtue, has something in common with the moral virtues, "for it is right judgment about things to be done"[24] and is therefore both an intellectual and a moral virtue.[25] The specific task of prudence is to find the just means in exercising the moral virtues:

> To be conformed to right reason is the proper purpose of any moral virtue. The intent of temperance is to prevent us straying from reason because of our lusts; of fortitude lest we forsake the judgment of right reason because of fear or rashness. Such an end is prescribed for us by our natural reason, which bids each to act according to reason. Yet quite how and through what we strike the virtuous mean, this is the business of prudence. For though keeping the mean is the aim of moral virtue, nevertheless it is in the correct marshalling of the means to the end that the mean is found.[26]

If the specific task of prudence is to find the just means in exercising the moral virtues, it therefore follows that this virtue does not have its own matter on which to act but is applied to the matter of the other moral virtues. Moreover, since prudence permanently enables the practical reason to judge and command at all times and with ease

---

24. I–II, q. 58, a. 3, ad 1, p. 71.

25. The Thomistic distinction between the intellectual virtues, which perfect the intellect, and the moral virtues, which perfect the "appetite" (in the sense of inclination, as Aquinas defines this term in I–II, q. 8, a. 1) derives from the Aristotelian distinction between dianoetic (intellectual) and ethic (moral) virtues.

26. *Summa Theologiae*, vol. 36 ("Prudence" (2a2ae, 47–56), T. Gilby, tr.), London and New York, 1974, II–II, q. 47, a. 7, p. 25.

what is morally good and dutiful in concrete situations, its seat is in the practical reason, the role of which is knowing the truth in view of practical action. In this role, practical reason is not only a guide for moral action (in which case prudence would be a condition for the virtues rather than itself a virtue) but is also the subject of moral action and virtues. Prudence resides in the cognitive faculty, because

> sight is of a cognitive, not an affective power.... And so it is clear that prudence is a function directly of a cognitive power. All the same that is not a sense-power, by which we know only objects offered here and now to empirical experience.... Prudence learns from the past and present about the future; this is the special office of reason, since it involves a process of comparison. Accordingly we are left with the conclusion that prudence precisely speaking is in the reason.[27]

In the end, according to Aquinas, prudence is the habitual disposition (acquired by repeated and virtuous acts) to make right judgments and give proper guidance in concrete cases, in any moral matter and circumstance. Without this virtuous stability in the concrete guidance of the moral life, that life would easily be at the whim of preferences prompted by the varied dispositions of the appetite.

If prudence is the moral virtue regulating the means, which is to say the most suitable actions for the concrete achievement of the good, ensuring upright discernment amid the instability of the many different circumstances of the practical life, it should therefore seek, judge, and impose the verdict of virtuous practical action.

In his doctrine on the human acts, in questions 6 to 21 of the I–II of the *Summa Theologica*, Thomas Aquinas analyzes the acts of the intellect and the will that come together in the formation of a moral act and distinguishes them by setting them in relation to the end, the means, and the execution of the act. The three acts proper

---

27. Ibid., a. 1, r., p. 5.

to prudence (the object of which is the means and not the ultimate end, which is not subject to its deliberations) are counsel, judgment, and command, all of which derive from the intellect. The specific and most important act proper to prudence is *imperium*, or "command":

> Assuming the definition of prudence as right reason applied to human conduct... then it follows that the chief act of prudence will be the chief act of reason as engaged with conduct. Here the activity of reason goes through three stages.... The first is taking counsel, which... is inquiry in order to discover. The second is forming a judgment on what has been discovered. So far we have not left theory. Practice, however, is another matter. For the practical reason, which is meant for the doing of something, pushes on to a third act, namely of commanding; this consists in bringing into execution what has been thought out and decided on. And because this approaches more closely to what the practical reason is for, it is a chief act of the practical reason, and so of prudence as well.[28]

Command is an act of reason under the impetus of the will.[29] A moral action, to be perfect, requires both the intellect and the will to be properly guided and ordered. Love is the first motion of the will and every appetite. In this sense, prudence is said to be love, "not that of its nature it is a kind of love, but because its activity is caused by love."[30]

The dynamics of a morally good act therefore appear to be quite complex and are influenced by both conscience and prudence. Thomas Aquinas, however, insists on the affirmation that prudence essentially emerges in the imperative function, which is necessarily

28. Ibid., a. 8, r., pp. 27 and 29.
29. "Setting in motion as such is a function of the will. But command implies a motioning together with a kind of ordinance. That is why it is an act of reason" (ibid., ad 3, p. 29).
30. Ibid., a. 1, ad 1, p. 7.

grafted into the dynamics of a concrete act. Being an act that follows a free choice, an act of prudence never remains in the sphere of knowledge alone but is found in the sphere of actions that have explicitly been contemplated and deliberated, even though it is formally exercised by reason. It is certainly based also on synderesis, which is the habit of knowledge from practical first principles and the basic core of conscience. However, while the dictates of the practical reason become concrete in the actual knowledge of the particular on the order of knowledge (conscience) alone, the first practical principles lead to honest moral action—the exercise of prudence—through the will, which in turn has to experience the appeal of the honest ends proper to the moral virtues in order to accept them. Aquinas also gives value to these functions of practical knowledge alone and undoubtedly attributes them to the conscience; however, he does not admit the existence of a moral life until those knowledge data reach the act of *"imperium rationis"* through the free decision of the will.

4. PRUDENCE IN SAINT THOMAS AQUINAS AND DISCRETION/PRUDENCE IN SAINT CATHERINE

As Deman has rightly pointed out, Aquinas "entrusts prudence with the task of perpetuating the constant and venerable tradition that discretion had carried through to him." In this manner, "prudence sets itself at the end of the reigning tradition of discretion. It inherits everything that the masters of the spiritual life had stored in this term."[31]

In comparing Aquinas's prudence with Catherine's discretion, the first common requirement to emerge is the knowledge of the truth. For Aquinas, prudence is the virtue that permanently guides the

---

31. Saint Thomas d'Aquin, *Somme Théologique*, "La Prudence" (T. Deman, ed.), Paris, 1947, Appendice II, pp. 407–8.

practical reason in judging and commanding what is morally good and binding in concrete situations. This implies that it is impossible to make a right judgment and a right moral decision without an effort of the reason to seek and love the truth,[32] which truth is present in the universal norm as well as the particular norm applicable to one's concrete situation. Aquinas distinguishes between speculative intelligence and practical reason: while both derive from the same faculty, which is the intellect, the former has the task of knowing the truth in its universal dimension, and the latter has the task of knowing the truth in view of a practical action. The virtue of prudence therefore presupposes knowledge of the truth: speculative knowledge that becomes, by extension, practical knowledge aimed at guiding the moral life. It is in the concrete action that the reason is involved in its executive dimension, by way of the three acts proper to prudence (counsel, judgment, and command), which all belong to the intellect.

Catherine's discretion/prudence, too, inasmuch as it is discernment, depends on true knowledge, which is therefore one of its essential conditions. Knowledge is true because it shows man the truth about himself and God, which are inseparable truths because knowing oneself means not only recognizing one's nothingness (since man derives his being from God) and the moral depravity of sin but also recognizing the divine "everything" and God's infinite mercy. It is this true knowledge that leads man to recognize that he has been created by God out of love "in his own image and likeness"[33] and recreated in the blood of Christ.

Catherine attributes a fundamental and indispensable function to the truth:[34] it is only by following the path of the knowledge of the

32. "At the end of his career as *Magister*, Thomas formulated his conviction and intention not to be anything else than a servant of the truth on God and on the things of God" (Y. Congar, "Saint Thomas, maître de vie spirituelle," in *Seminarium* 29 (1977), pp. 994–1007, at p. 1001).

33. Letter 13: *Letters*, IV, p. 18 (*Lettere*, I, p. 44).

34. According to G. Cavallini, truth is the "substance" of the *Dialogue*, and it is no wonder that, of the sixteen letters Catherine addressed to Raymond of Capua, eight have truth as their explicit theme, while several others have it as their implicit theme (Introduction to *Dialogo*, p. xxxii, including footnote 24).

truth that one can successfully and effectively practice what is good. One of the most frequently recurring appeals, in Catherine's writings, is precisely to vest oneself with the truth. This is her invocation at the end of the *Dialogue*:

> Clothe, clothe me with yourself, eternal Truth, so that I may run the course of this mortal life in true obedience and in the light of most holy faith. With that light I sense my soul once again becoming drunk! Thanks be to God! Amen.[35]

It is the truth that sets us free. But we cannot have this truth perfectly unless we know it, "for unless we know it we cannot love it, and unless we love it we will neither discover it within ourselves nor follow it."[36]

Knowing the truth means first of all recognizing that human beings are creatures incapable of giving themselves their own being, from which it follows that they are ontologically dependent on God. As Catherine often repeats when invoking God, the "first sweet Truth," he is the One who is, without whom we are not.[37] Catherine's teachings take their cue from these two axioms, namely that God is the supreme being who gives life to all that is and that what is created has its being by way of participation. God is the "Creator of everything that has any share in being," and sin, not being of his making, is nonbeing.[38]

This profound reflection on God's being and man's ontological dependence reveals some clear affinity between Catherine and Aquinas. Furthermore, for Catherine, man depends on God not only in his being but also in his knowledge of the truth: God is the uncreated being and absolute truth such that, if being means for human creatures participating in God's being, then knowing the truth means participating in the truth that is God.[39] Additionally, knowledge of

---

35. *Dialogue*, p. 366, ch. 167 (*Dialogo*, p. 587).
36. Letter 284: *Letters*, III, p. 115 (*Lettere*, IV, p. 202).
37. Letter 66: *Letters* I, p. 157 (*Lettere*, I, p. 252).
38. *Dialogue*, p. 56, ch. 18 (*Dialogo*, p. 56).
39. For Aquinas, as for Catherine, God is the highest being, the highest truth, and the highest good. There is only one ontological truth whereby all things are true,

the truth cannot be attained through natural reason alone, as the latter must be enlightened by the light of faith. This theme, too, which is found very frequently in Catherine's writings, is close to Aquinas's teaching. In the *Dialogue*, one reads that nobody can walk in the way of the truth without the light of reason that comes from God, true Light. In addition, however, there is a need for the light of faith that is received in baptism. If man exercises this faith "by virtue with the light of reason, reason will in turn be enlightened by faith," and this faith will give life and lead man in the way of truth. This is the light that allows man to reach the true Light and without which man remains in darkness.[40]

Once man knows the truth with the light of reason enlightened by faith, he loves it because the soul always longs for the good by its very nature. This is why Catherine writes, in the *Dialogue*, that in the supernatural light men love God, because love follows upon understanding: "[t]he more they know, the more they love, and the more they love, the more they know."[41]

Knowledge of the truth cannot but lead to a movement toward the good that is God: "[t]hose who do not know cannot love, and those who know also love."[42] This close connection between knowledge and love also demonstrates a certain affinity with the Thomistic principle, inherited from Augustine, according to which "one cannot love anything other than what one knows."[43] Likewise, for Catherine, one can attain the good only by knowing the truth.[44]

and there is only one goodness (God) from whom all beings draw their perfection by participation.

40. *Dialogue*, pp. 184–85, ch. 98 (*Dialogo*, pp. 270–71). See also *Letters*, IV, p. 17 (*Lettere*, I, p. 42).

41. *Dialogue*, p. 157, ch. 85 (*Dialogo*, p. 226).

42. Letter 77: *Letters*, II, p. 75 (*Lettere*, II, p. 24).

43. "Love ranks above knowledge as an impulse towards an object, but knowledge is above love in holding it; Augustine says, *None is beloved unless known*" (*Summa Theologiae*, vol. 16 ("Purpose and happiness" (1a2ae, 1–5), T. Gilby, tr.), London and New York, 1969, I–II, q. 3, a. 4, ad 4, p. 73).

44. This is expressly stated at the beginning of the *Dialogue*, in the opening passage that was earlier quoted in its entirety (*Dialogue*, p. 25; *Dialogo*, p. 1).

Last, there is a certain affinity between Aquinas and Catherine in the primacy assigned to prudence in the moral action. Aquinas devotes an entire question to the connection between the virtues, with the aim of explaining the unity and coherence of the moral life as a whole. Regarding prudence, he writes that "no moral virtue can be possessed without prudence" because it is proper to moral virtue to make a right choice. But to make a right choice it is not enough to have a right end: one also needs the right means to that end, which is precisely "the work of prudence", which counsels, judges, and commands in this field. Conversely, one cannot have prudence unless one has the moral virtues, because "prudence is right reason about things to be done, and its starting point is what this is for, to which end a man is rightly disposed by moral virtue. Hence, just as speculative science cannot be possessed without an understanding of principles, so neither can prudence without the moral virtues."[45] The connection between prudence and the other virtues could not be explained more clearly.[46]

For Aquinas, prudence is the guiding virtue of the moral life because it constitutes the concrete rule and just measure of every virtuous action. To achieve its purpose without degenerating into vice, the impulse itself driving toward the ends of the moral virtues needs the just measure set by prudence. In Catherine, while one hardly finds a systematic treatment of the virtues, the expression "true solid virtues" ("Love never stands alone, but has as her companions all the true solid virtues, because all the virtues have life from charity's love")[47] mirrors Aquinas's thought.

45. *Summa Theologiae*, vol. 23 ("Virtue" (1a2ae, 55–67), W. D. Hughes, tr.), op. cit., I–II, q. 65, a. 1, r., pp. 181–82.

46. In Aquinas, there is a dual foundation to the connection of the moral virtues: the means (*medium virtutis*) brought about by prudence, and the end, which is the principle of the moral life.

47. *Dialogue*, p. 328, ch. 154 (*Dialogo*, p. 523).

For Catherine as well as Aquinas, discretion has its roots in charity, even though it is a "seasoning" of all the virtues. Charity remains the source of every virtue and "in Catherine's dictations it takes the form of a root, sprouting and frondescent in the 'tree of love' that presents the doctrine of the virtues in a different perspective: the perspective of 'discretion.'"[48] In fact, the "child" of discretion emerges from the side of the base of the trunk of this "tree of love," such that every fruit produced by this tree is seasoned with discretion, "and this unites them all."[49]

5. CONCLUSION

The similarities between Aquinas's virtue of prudence and Catherine's discretion/prudence seem to indicate that Catherine had some knowledge, however indirect, of the thinking of Saint Thomas Aquinas. While it is not plausible to assume that Catherine ever read Thomas's writings, of which no vernacular translations were circulating during her time, it is feasible to imagine that some of the inspiring principles of Thomistic doctrine reached her through the Dominican environment with which she was familiar in Siena.[50] Perhaps Giuliana Cavallini hit the nail on the head when she affirmed that the "harmonies" between Catherine and Aquinas are above all

48. G. Cavallini, "Consonanze tomistiche nel linguaggio cateriniano. Le vere e reali virtù," in *Rassegna di Ascetica e Mistica*—"*S. Caterina da Siena*" 1 (1974), pp. 73–82, at p. 81.

49. *Dialogue*, p. 42, ch. 10 (*Dialogo*, p. 31).

50. This is also the conclusion reached by G. D'Urso, according to whom some of Catherine's thought may be closer to Thomas's commentaries on the sentences of Peter Lombard than the *Summa Theologica*, by virtue of the influence on her of such preachers as Passavanti, Adimari, Jacopo Cini, or Dominici, who were familiar with Lombard's sentences. The research of the exact sources remains complicated, though, because in general the Dominican writers of the thirteenth and fourteenth centuries "were not, strictly speaking, Thomists, but rather eclectics" (*Il genio di santa Caterina*, Roma, 1971, p. 177). On this point, see also M. W. Flood, "St. Thomas's Thought in the *Dialogue* of St. Catherine," in *Spirituality Today* 32 (1980), pp. 25–35. That the preachers may have acted as a filter between Thomas and Catherine finds indirect

indications of a unique spiritual affinity between the two saints. It is an affinity whose roots are deeply planted in that "first sweet Truth" that shaped each of them, and in which the mind of Catherine—like the mind of "glorious Thomas"—reflected upon itself and derived an entirely luminous and sure teaching: the doctrine of the Truth.[51]

confirmation in C. Delcorno, when he notes that, in Italy, "preaching to the laity was undertaken in the vernacular from the thirteenth century, and only under exceptional circumstances in Latin" ("Medieval Preaching in Italy (1200–1500)," in B. M. Kienzle (ed.), *The Sermon*, Turnhout, 2000, pp. 449–560, at p. 494).

51. G. Cavallini, "Consonanze tomistiche nel linguaggio cateriniano," op. cit., p. 82.

Chapter 10

Domenico Cavalca and Some Contemporaries of Catherine

1. INTRODUCTION

The preceding chapter sought to provide a glimpse of the richness of the doctrinal fabric, derived from the Patristic and Scholastic traditions, that emerges from Catherine's reflection on discretion. It is highly improbable that this doctrinal richness was the result of direct access to the classical sources in the Christian tradition because Catherine had only a very limited understanding of Latin. It therefore seems reasonable to assume that the transmission of these sources must have occured largely within the context of an oral tradition, mediated by the occasions offered to Catherine by experience: homilies, changes of location, travel, and above all intense and constant interaction with the members of her community.

The heterogeneous nature of Catherine's community was already mentioned earlier: important representatives of the Dominican order such as Raymond of Capua, Caffarini, and Bartolomeo Dominici were also accompanied by Franciscans like Gabriele da Volterra and Lazzarino da Pisa, the Augustinian William Flete, and the Vallombrosan Giovanni delle Celle. Additionally, Catherine's closest disciples included the Sienese notary Cristofano di Gano Guidini, the erudite Stefano di Corrado Maconi, the poet Neri di Landoccio de' Pagliaresi, and Barduccio di Piero Canigiani. Within this varied community, the influence of Dominican spirituality was certain, if

COMPARISON IN HISTORICAL PERSPECTIVE

one also considers that the homilies at Saint Dominic's church in Siena constituted an important source for Catherine's reflection.

Alongside the oral tradition, scholars agree that, within the Dominican tradition, Domenico Cavalca's *The Mirror of the Cross* must have been a direct source, all the more so as it was written in the vernacular. This little book, which Catherine could easily have accessed given its wide dissemination, is regarded by some as one of the most important sources of Catherine's thinking.[1]

2. THE MIRROR OF THE CROSS BY DOMENICO CAVALCA

In the Italian literature, Domenico Cavalca[2] is primarily remembered among early prose writers for his most famous work, *The Mirror of the Cross*, which was written in the vernacular to facilitate catechetical and ascetic instruction for those who did not understand Latin.

Are there points of contact between this work and Catherine's teaching on discretion, both in its aspect of discernment ("light" and "knowledge") and of the practical fulfillment of discernment ("rendering the debt")? To answer this question, it is necessary to recall a few passages from *The Mirror of the Cross*.[3]

1. According to G. D'Urso, "St. Catherine was certainly familiar with Cavalca's translation of the *Lives of the Holy Fathers*, of which she retained facts and thoughts.... Undoubtedly she read and deeply assimilated *The Mirror of the Cross*, borrowing many basic ideas for her own reflection; no other book left more visible traces in Catherine's writings" (*Il genio di santa Caterina*, op. cit., p. 119).

2. On Domenico Cavalca (circa 1270–1342), see B. M. Ashley, "Dominic Cavalca and a Spirituality of the Word," available at http://domcentral.org/dominic-cavalca-and-a-spirituality-of-the-word.

3. As there is no English translation of this work (at least to the author's knowledge), the page references here are to this Italian edition: D. Cavalca, *Lo Specchio della Croce* (T. S. Centi, ed.), Bologna, 1992.

Cavalca tends to prefer the term *discretion*[4] over the term *prudence*, which is found only once in the limited sense of human prudence, in chapter 45, when reporting the passage from Matthew 11:25, where Jesus praises the Father for having hidden from the "prudent" and the learned what he has revealed to the childlike.[5]

In chapter 35, Cavalca presents discretion as the science to which belongs the rational knowledge of temporal things, namely "having discretion between evil and good, between better and worse, and recognizing evil and the dangers where we are."[6] To obtain this science, one must invoke it:

> Give us therefore, oh Christ on the cross, this science, give us discretion, and show us that our danger is great, and that many are the evils of this world, which lead us to death; and give us the discretion to know how to use the temporal goods in that way in which you used them in your life.[7]

This passage reveals discretion in its entirety, which is both discernment between good and evil and its concrete fulfillment in using the temporal things similarly to how Christ used them in his earthly life. Hence both aspects of discretion are present in *The Mirror of the Cross*. The discerning aspect is encountered primarily in the twofold knowledge of oneself and of God, as in Catherine's writings, since discretion as discernment depends on the knowledge of this truth. In this way, the cross is seen as a mirror in which one knows everything, "namely God in his goodness, power and wisdom; our state in its guilt and dignity."[8]

---

4. The term *discretion* occurs in chs. 9 (p. 84), 26 (p. 206), 35 (pp. 276 and 278), 50 (p. 404); the adverb *discreetly* in the Prologue (p. 24); *indiscreetly* in ch. 47 (p. 376); and the adjective *discretive/discreet* in chs. 10 (p. 94) and 47 (p. 376).

5. Ibid., p. 360, ch. 45.

6. Ibid., p. 276, ch. 35.

7. Ibid.

8. Ibid., p. 244, ch. 30.

The three attributes of God (power, wisdom, and goodness), which are so often found in Catherine's writings on the Father, the Son, and the Holy Spirit, are also found in the passage by Cavalca that has just been quoted. In chapter 30, on the other hand, Cavalca discusses the three faculties of the soul (which are so familiar to Catherine) through which Christ, from the cross, attracts man's soul as if Christ said:

> this exaltation, i.e. this cross in which I will be exalted from the earth, will be so efficacious, and with so much virtue, that I will draw to myself the heart of man with all its power and movement. I will attract the intellect that it may think at me; the will that it may love me; and the memory that it may never forget me.[9]

This knowledge of God and self is the most useful and necessary kind that man can attain, which is why Saint Augustine prays God that he may make us know him and know ourselves: this "useful knowledge Christ gave us on the cross."[10] The other aspect of discretion, namely rendering the debt, can also be found in *The Mirror of the Cross*, particularly in reference to the debt of love due to God. On this, Cavalca writes that we cannot have Christ's first perfection, which is loving God gratuitously, "as we are bound to love him because of our debt," on account of the goodness and love that he has shown us.[11]

This brief comparison between the two authors shows that it is plausible to suppose a certain influence of *The Mirror of the Cross* on Catherine's thinking, at least with regard to discretion. At the same time, the comparison draws out how Catherine develops this notion more extensively and how deeper her thinking is.[12] The same can be

---

9. Ibid., p. 30, ch. 1.
10. Ibid., p. 228, ch. 29.
11. Ibid., p. 60, ch. 6.
12. From a comparison between Catherine's *Dialogue* and Cavalca's *The Mirror of the Cross*, G. D'Urso has concluded that the latter work was for Catherine "the work of a manual laborer by comparison with the drawings of a great architect" (*Il genio di santa Caterina*, op. cit., p. 68).

said of the influence on Catherine by Cavalca's vernacular translation of the *Lives of the Fathers*. She was certainly familiar with this work, as she attests in two passages of the *Dialogue*.[13] At the same time, even when referring to the discernment of visions, with respect to which she may have been inspired by some of the passages dedicated to Saint Anthony of the desert in Cavalca's translation, Catherine's deep reflection goes well beyond its model.

In conclusion, Cavalca's writings may have been a source of Catherine's exposition on discretion, but still a minor one, in the sense of offering no more than raw materials for her original and profound meditation.

Cavalca was not the only author of the fourteenth century dealing with discretion and prudence, which is why Bridget of Sweden, John Colombini, and Raymond of Capua are next briefly mentioned.

3. DISCRETION AND PRUDENCE IN SAINT BRIDGET OF SWEDEN

Saint Bridget of Sweden's[14] book of *Revelations* ("*Liber caelestis revelationum Dei*")[15] is the mystical work that best reflects her spirituality, which is of Cistercian roots and centers entirely on the passion of Christ and devotion to Mary. Bridget experienced her revelations from Christ and the Virgin Mary while in a state of ecstasy: after

13. See *Dialogue*, pp. 291–92, ch. 141 (*Dialogo*, p. 456); *Dialogue*, pp. 357–58, ch. 165 (*Dialogo*, p. 574).

14. On the life and spirituality of Bridget of Sweden (circa 1303–1373), see M. T. Harris (ed.), *Birgitta of Sweden. Life and Selected Revelations*, New York and Mahwah, NJ, 1990; C. L. Sahlin, *Birgitta of Sweden and the Voice of Prophecy*, Woodbridge, 2001.

15. The first complete translation of the *Revelations* into English is under way. At the time of writing, only three volumes have been published: *The Revelations of St. Birgitta of Sweden* (B. Morris, ed., D. Searby, tr.), Oxford and New York, 2006 (*Volume I: Liber Caelestis, Books I–III*), 2008 (*Volume II: Liber Caelestis, Books IV–V*), and 2012 (*Volume III: Liber Caelestis, Books VI–VII*).

awakening, she would write them down personally or dictate them in Swedish to her confessor, who later translated them into Latin.

Bridget's mission had a rather specific aim: aiding the poor and unhappy and urging the Church and lay leaders toward greater responsibility and reflection in God's name. As Catherine of Siena would later do, Bridget exhorted the popes to return to Rome. More specifically, she exhorted three popes in vain to return from Avignon to Rome, and their premature deaths were later connected to the warnings she had pronounced about what would happen if they did not return to Rome.[16]

Her *Liber caelestis* contains many revelations with apocalyptic content and others presented with complex allegories. In this concise investigation, only some of the passages from the *Liber caelestis* (or *Revelations*) containing the terms *discretion* and *prudence* are examined. In book 2, the Virgin Mary talks about "those Jews and pagans who would like to be Christians, if they only knew how,"[17] saying that they would pronounce this invocation addressed to Christ:

So come, kind Lord! We would like to give ourselves to you, because we understand that in you there is love for souls, the [discreet] use of all things, perfect purity, and life everlasting.[18]

This passage, in which Bridget attributes to Christ the discreet use of all things, brings to mind those passages in which Catherine refers to the "prudence" of God.

The Swedish saint instead speaks about prudence in book 2 of the *Revelations*. In chapter 6, Christ is represented as a king on the battlefield with the Christians to his right and the pagans to his left. He rejects the Christians, for whom he had prepared "an eternal reward,"

16. Clement VI died in December 1352; his successor, Innocent VI, in 1362. Urban V then returned to Rome in 1367, but, despite Bridget's prophecy announcing he would shortly die, he went back to Avignon where he died in 1370. It was Gregory XI, elected in December 1370, who would bring back the papacy to Rome.

17. *The Revelations, Volume I*, op. cit., p. 183, ch. 3 (line 47).

18. Ibid., pp. 183–84, ch. 3 (line 52).

because they had thrown down "the helmets of God's will and the weapons of virtue," and this

> has so blinded them that the apertures of the helmets through which they should be able to see are at the back of their heads and in front of them is darkness....What do these apertures in the helmets represent if not the consideration of the future and [prudence] and circumspection of present realities?[19]

The explanation of the two holes in the helmet immediately follows in the text: the "delight of future rewards and the horrors of future punishments" come from the first hole ("the consideration of the future"), while "how much they may have transgressed God's commandments and how they should improve" come from the second ("prudence and circumspection of present realities").[20]

In chapter 21 of book 2, Bridget relays the words of the Virgin Mary on the soul that is "married to its God" and, upon hearing the words of divine mercy, comes to understand three things:

> First, that it [i.e. the soul] should [be prudent] lest, the higher it rose and the more it relied on perishable things, the worse would be the fall that threatened it. Second, it understood that there was nothing in the world but sorrow and care. Third, that its reward from the devil would be evil.[21]

Last, the adverb *prudently* is found in the words of Christ to a sinful king in book 8:

> I bestowed on you a considerable grace; in fact, I showed you my will, how you must behave in your regime and how you have to do it honestly and prudently.[22]

19. Ibid., p. 189, ch. 6 (lines 11, 14, and 15–16).
20. Ibid., p. 189, ch. 6 (lines 17–18).
21. Ibid., p. 230, ch. 21 (line 33).
22. As book 8 is not yet available in the complete English translation that is currently under way, this passage was translated by the author from *Ciò che disse Cristo a Santa Brigida. Le rivelazioni. Antologia*, Cinisello Balsamo, 2002, p. 214, ch. 56.

In conclusion, Bridget refers to prudence as the virtue that is necessary for living morally and attaining eternal salvation. In her writings, one perceives the power of prophecy and of the moral exhortations that she addresses to princes and pontiffs, whom she does not spare from harsh admonitions even on the subject of moral reform among the Christian people and the clergy themselves. In her reflections, however, one does not find that in-depth analysis of the notions of discretion and prudence that instead characterizes Catherine's works.

4. KNOWLEDGE OF SELF AND GOD, DISCRETION AND PRUDENCE IN JOHN COLOMBINI

John Colombini[23] was a distant relative and near contemporary of Saint Catherine of Siena.[24] His only writings are letters of which it has been written that, despite their appearance of being "so simple, lacking a deliberate form and scientific approach, they are authentic treatises on mysticism."[25]

Trained at the school of the Franciscan Friars Minor in Siena and influenced by Franciscan teachings, Colombini focused his apostolic work on stirring everyone to love and honor "Jesus Christ Crucified." Charity is at the heart of all his letters: charity to God, to oneself, and to one's neighbor. For him, charity joined with poverty and prayer should serve to help one come to know and love God. From time to

---

23. John Colombini (1304–1367), born to a noble Sienese family, was the founder of the congregation of the Gesuati. See, in English translation, the classic F. Belcari, *The Life of B. Giov. Colombini*, London, 1874 (translated from the editions of 1541 and 1832).

24. "Lisa Colombini, sister-in-law of the Saint, was a cousin of the Blessed. Tommaso di Guelfaccio, converted by Colombini...was one of Catherine's disciples. When Colombini died, Catherine was twenty years old" (B. G. Colombini, *Le lettere* (P. Cherubelli, ed.), Siena, 1957, p. 13, note 14).

25. Ibid., p. 6.

time, Colombini refers to knowledge in a way that closely resembles Catherine's true knowledge, which is the fundamental requirement of discretion in Catherine. In one letter, Colombini invokes the "compassionate and kind God" to have "a light of truth," whereby we may know that all the goods are from him and likewise know that by ourselves we cannot bring about anything good.[26]

Colombini then discusses the effect of this twofold knowledge in letter 80, when writing that the soul wishes to suffer and be persecuted "because it knows God's bounty and its own cowardice and misery."[27] In letter 13, Colombini relates knowledge to debt (a recurring theme in Catherine's writings, as was seen earlier). This is Colombini's text:

> Irrespective of how much virtue is in us, we cannot attribute it to ourselves, but we are rather indebted to God for it; the greater the virtue, the greater our debt and obligation ... the greater the knowledge, the greater the debt.[28]

Knowledge and light,[29] which are necessary to become "true servants of Christ and true and pure Christians," can only come from God, which is why Colombini invokes Christ so that he may give everyone "true knowledge and eternal life" and enlighten us with the light of the Holy Spirit.[30] Then, in letter 105, Colombini derives from the "light of discretion" the perfect knowledge of the truth to which a soul married to Christ may aspire.[31] Aside from this passage, though, Colombini rarely mentions discretion.

26. Ibid., letter 1, p. 38.
27. Ibid., letter 80, p. 241.
28. Ibid., letter 13, p. 82. Other references to paying the "debt" and to the "obligation" to love God are in letters 10 (p. 75), 15 (p. 88), and 62 (p. 201).
29. Ibid., letter 98, p. 278.
30. Ibid., letter 46, p. 170. Other references to "knowledge" are in letters 5 (p. 56), 15 (p. 91), 57 (p. 192), and 62 (p. 202).
31. Ibid., letter 105, p. 292.

In letter 4, he urges a "wise and discreet" penance.[32] In letter 101, still referring to discretion in the sense of just measure, he states that "by an excess of fervor" one "passes beyond reason and discretion."[33] In letter 47, on the other hand, discretion has the meaning of tact and gentleness.[34]

As to prudence, Colombini generally tends to use this term alongside "wisdom," as in his exhortation to become "wise and prudent," which can be found in letters 9, 64, and 72.[35] The two terms are found together again in letter 7 but with a rather ironic and negative connotation.[36] Letter 48 is of greater interest, as in it prudence is used in reference to Christ: "trusting in the blessed Christ and in prudence and virtue of this holy Lord."[37]

In conclusion, the notion of knowledge of self and God is present in Colombini's letters, at times alongside the notion of rendering the debt. The use of the terms *discretion* and *prudence* instead appears to be minor, even though Colombini's attribution of prudence to Christ introduces an element of analogy with Catherine's divine prudence.

5. THE *LEGENDA MAIOR* BY RAYMOND OF CAPUA

The *Legenda maior*,[38] which was written by Raymond of Capua,[39] Catherine's confessor with whom she had a profound spiritual friendship,[40] is considered the official biography of Saint Catherine.

---

32. Ibid., letter 4, p. 53.
33. Ibid., letter 101, p. 284.
34. Ibid., letter 47, p. 171.
35. Ibid., letters 9 (p. 70), 64 (p. 212), and 72 (p. 225).
36. "wise and prudent and much learned" (ibid., letter 7, p. 62).
37. Ibid., letter 48, p. 174.
38. For the original Latin text, see "S. Catharinae Senensis Vita (auctore Raimundo Capuano)," in *Acta Sanctorum Aprilis* III, Parisiis et Romae, 1866, pp. 862–969.
39. See the brief bibliographical note provided in chapter 1.
40. See P. M. Conner, "Catherine of Siena and Raymond of Capua—Enduring Friends," in *Studia Mystica* 12 (1989), pp. 22–29.

In chapter 3 of book 2 of his work, the Dominican friar attributes to Catherine the "gift of discretion":

> Catherine now began not so much to give away her father's property as to scatter it wholesale. And yet, since discretion was one of her outstanding virtues, she did not make an object of her generosity simply of everyone who asked, but only of those whom she knew herself to be really in need, including also those needy ones who did not ask.[41]

In Raymond of Capua, as in Catherine, the terms *discretion* and *prudence* are synonyms. The Dominican friar writes that, in her childhood, Catherine had "[prudently] resolved not to quench the Spirit."[42] Then, when she reached the age of discretion and announced that she had taken a vow of virginity, her family members discovered that the girl, who had until then been silent and reserved, had grown bold "to speak her mind in [prudent] words well weighed and straight to the point."[43] In book 2, recalling what the saint had told him about the passion of Christ, Raymond writes:

> Thoughts such as these, expressed in words at once well-chosen and rich in meaning, formed the substance of the instructions [of the very prudent virgin] on the passion of our Lord and Saviour.[44]

In summary, Raymond of Capua, too, uses the terms *discretion* and *prudence* in his *Legenda maior* and does so similarly to what Catherine had done in her writings.

41. *Life*, p. 126 (para. 131).
42. Ibid., p. 35 (para. 35).
43. Ibid., p. 51 (para. 55).
44. Ibid., pp. 200–201 (para. 212).

6. CONCLUSION

The brief analysis of the last three authors considered in this chapter brings to light certain analogies to Catherine's language. Discretion and prudence are synonyms in these authors, too. Furthermore, the "discreet use of all things" that Saint Bridget of Sweden attributes to Christ and the prudence of the Lord mentioned by Blessed John Colombini closely recall three passages in which Catherine makes reference to the prudence of God. This is also true of the pairing of the notion of "understanding" and "debt" in Colombini's letters, taking up a recurring theme in Catherine's works.

* * *

What are therefore the results of the study conducted in this third part? First of all, the brief investigation of the Christian tradition preceding Catherine has confirmed that, while it is possible to find passages in her writings that refer back to discernment in the sense of *discretio spirituum*, in reality, Catherine's discretion includes not only the meaning of discernment but also the fulfillment of what has been recognized as just and must be fulfilled in practice, in accordance with proper measure and moderation. In this respect, Catherine truly follows in the footsteps of the tradition that preceded her. However, while *discretio* (and later the virtue of prudence) is just one among many themes for the major authors in this tradition, discretion takes on an entirely unique importance in Catherine's works, characterizing all of her writings and becoming the pivotal core of her spirituality.

A second result of this study is that, even after Aquinas's synthesis of the tradition of *discretio* with prudence, the use of the term *discretion* did not die out, but continued to be used as a synonym of prudence by some spiritual writers who were Catherine's contemporaries.

PART IV

SYNTHESIS

Discretion between Mysticism and Morality

The mystical aspect of Catherine's teaching is acknowledged by all those who have studied her writings, which is why her name is listed among those of the greatest mystics of the fourteenth century. Pope Paul VI, in the homily that followed his proclamation of Saint Catherine as a Doctor of the Church, stated:

> what strikes us most about the Saint is her infused wisdom. That is to say, lucid, profound and inebriating absorption of the divine truths and the mysteries of the faith contained in the Holy Books of the Old and New Testaments. That assimilation was certainly favoured by most singular natural gifts, but it was also evidently something prodigious, due to a charism of wisdom from the Holy Spirit, a mystic charism.[1]

Her state of ecstasy (one of the most powerful moments of any mystical experience) was attested by her disciples. In describing it when dictating the Dialogue, Raymond of Capua writes vividly of the suspension of all her

---

1. "Pope Paul VI Confers Title on Siena Mystic, October 4th," in *L'Osservatore Romano* (English edn., October 15, 1970), pp. 6–7, at p. 6.

senses.[2] Letter 373 is of great interest in this regard. In it, Catherine recounts one of her personal experiences to Raymond of Capua regarding a crisis she experienced in late January 1380:

> it seemed to me as if my soul had left my body...my soul seemed like something that had been set aside, since it didn't seem to be in my body; instead I was seeing my body as if it had been someone else.... I could see no way to move its tongue or any other part of it except as one might move a lifeless corpse. So I let my body lie just as it was, and kept my understanding fixed on the abyss of the Trinity.[3]

This estrangement of the soul from the body, this odd splitting, can perhaps convey what Catherine means when alluding to ecstasy. In any event, without even considering ecstasy and the levitations that some of her disciples mention, Catherine's writings themselves reveal this mystical aspect.[4] Her thought seems indeed to depend on a unique form of inspiration, which is expressed in all her writings and gives them a unified character. It is therefore possible to trace the Letters, the Dialogue, and the Prayers back to that same source of mystical inspiration,[5] which is examined in this final part from the limited perspective of discretion. In particular, chapter 11 addresses the specificity of Catherine's mysticism and the language in which it is expressed, and chapter 12 summarizes several considerations on the importance, originality, and unifying role of discretion in her doctrine.

---

2. See *Life*, pp. 309–10 (para. 332).

3. *Letters*, IV, p. 366 (*Lettere*, V, pp. 286–87).

4. "Her teaching does not reflect theological speculation: it is in the authentic tradition of Christian mysticism, from the Gospel, St Paul and St John, through St Augustine and St Bernard, to St Francis of Assisi" (J. Leclercq, F. Vandenbroucke, and L. Bouyer, *The Spirituality of the Middle Ages*, New York, 1982, pp. 411–12).

5. On this basis, G. Getto affirms that "among the first letters, the Dialogue, and the last letters, there are no changes of substance....The mysticism of the saint is refined in all these pages....A real difference does not exist, therefore, among the saint's writings" (*Letteratura religiosa del trecento*, op. cit., pp. 166–70).

Chapter 11

Catherine's Reflection as an Example of Supernatural Christian Mysticism

1. INTRODUCTION

If one were to summarize in general terms the main features of Catholic mysticism, a first problem to arise would be that the term *mysticism*, so often used since the nineteenth century and more often abused, has multiple meanings.[1] In the 1920s, Inge listed at least twenty-six different definitions of the word *mysticism*.[2] Sixty years later, Egan wrote that the number of definitions is in fact on the order of hundreds.[3] The picture is further complicated by the use of the term *mystic*, which was initially used as an adjective and later, starting in the seventeenth century, as a noun in its own right.

The adjective *mystical* (*mysticus* in Latin and *mystikós* in Greek) traces its origins to the religious sphere and specifically to the context of the so-called mystery cults in the Roman Empire between the early centuries before Christ and the first centuries after his coming. *Mystical* is the adjective of *mystery* (*mysterium* in Latin and *mystérion*

---

1. Likewise polysemic is the term *spirituality*. See, for example, what one reads in J.-P. Torrell, *Théologie et spiritualité suivi de Confessions d'un "thomiste,"* Paris, 2009, pp. 13 and 32–36.
2. W. R. Inge, *Christian Mysticism*, London, 1921.
3. H. Egan, *What Are They Saying about Mysticism?* New York, 1982.

in Greek), meaning "what one is silent about," since *mystérion* in turn derives from the Greek verb *myo*, meaning "I keep silent." This keeping silence may have a twofold motivation: either the impossibility of speaking about the mystical subject due to its ineffable qualities or the duty to keep silent to prevent the profane—those who are not able or ready to know the mystery—from profaning it. The term *mystérion* was later adopted by Saint Paul to express the content of Christian doctrine and the divine reality with which it brings one into communion. The Apostle of the Gentiles adopted this term from the language of pagan mysteries because they offered the possibility to those who were initiated of uniting with the deity and participating in the deity's life. Christianity likewise offered this perspective of participation in divine life through participation in the life of Christ and the Holy Spirit.[4] Saint Paul also uses the term *mystérion* to indicate the sacraments,[5] in particular the sacrament of marriage.

Mysticism, as it appeared historically in the understandings and practices of the Greco-Roman mystery religions of the first centuries before and after Christ, has been defined as natural (a form of union with God obtained through the use of natural strengths and in response to a natural need of communion with God) to distinguish it from supernatural mysticism, which is specifically Christian.

2. CHRISTIAN MYSTICISM AS SUPERNATURAL MYSTICISM

Christian mysticism is supernatural because it can only be grounded in the grace of Christ, which allows human nature to overcome itself to attain true participation in the life of God. In traditional Catholic language, the grace that causes mystical experience is called "operative grace" (*gratia operans*) as different from "cooperative grace"

---

4. See Romans 11:25 and 16:25–27; Ephesians 1:9, 3:3–5, and 3:9; Colossians 1:26; 2 Thessalonians 2:7; 1 Timothy 3:9 and 3:16.
5. See Ephesians 5:32.

(*gratia cooperans*), which is the grace of common exercise of the virtues, including the theological ones. The grace of mystical experience is called operative because it moves the will, which executes a free and responsible action (the act of mystical union) without the self-movement of the will, which instead occurs in the common exercise of the will outside of mystical experiences.

Christian mystical experience involves an intimate union with the trinitarian God thanks to the movements of the gifts of the Holy Spirit (particularly that of wisdom), which produce a union with the mystery of God and the contemplation of this mystery. In Christian mysticism, moreover, the humanity of the mystic does not dissolve itself into the divinity because grace does not substitute for nature but rather respects and ennobles it. A fundamental prerequisite for mystical experiences is total devotion of oneself to God, namely self-denial, which is obtained through obedience to the divine will, eliminating all that is opposed to God, starting with pride. Exercising humility and obeying God's will demonstrate that the necessary disciplining of one's selfishness and passions has been achieved. Self-denial finds various expressions in mystical language, such as "hatred of oneself," "stripping off oneself," and "dying to oneself." The mystical life involves two fundamental forms that correspond to the two faculties of the intellect and the will. Cognitive mystical experiences are called "mystical" or "infused contemplation";[6] affective mystical experiences are called "mystical union."

3. CATHERINE'S MYSTICISM AND ITS LANGUAGE

The charism of the wisdom of the Holy Spirit, which is the "mystical charism" of which Pope Paul VI spoke in his proclamation of Saint

---

6. "Mystical contemplation is a supernatural contemplative act, based on the knowledge of faith, animated by charity, and caused by the enlightenment of the Holy Spirit deriving from the gift of wisdom" (G. M. Cavalcoli, "Il silenzio della parola. Le mistiche a confronto," *Sacra doctrina* 47 (2002, Nos. 3–4), pp. 3–357, at p. 91).

Catherine as a Doctor of the Church, truly sheds light on Catherine's mysticism, which is a clear example of Christian mysticism grounded in supernatural grace.

Catherine's language expresses a coherent idea, which is deeply rooted in the truths of faith,[7] and proves the authenticity of the saint's mystical experiences, which are presented not as vague spiritual experiences or irrational darkness but as profound and personal understanding of the revealed truths.[8] This love of the truth, a product of her mystical experience, drove Catherine to share and love the eternal Truth in spite of the humble judgment she expressed on herself in letter 2:

> Know that of myself there is nothing to see or tell except utter poverty; I am ignorant and quite dull-witted. Everything else is from supreme eternal Truth, so give the credit to him, not to me.[9]

It is her love of the truth that spurred Catherine to teach spiritual and moral ways in a concrete manner, with great effort and sincerity. This is evident in all her writings, especially in the letters that Catherine wrote to unbelievers and hardened sinners, in which ethical and spiritual themes predominate. The zeal for communicating the truths that she learned and explored in the depth of her mystical experiences is reflected in Catherine's dictations, which have an eminently parenetic tone. The saint was not at all concerned with the

---

7. Catherine's mysticism "is an expression of Scripture and Catholic dogma" (G. Berceville, "Le chemin de Vérité. Principes et étapes de la vie spirituelle selon Catherine de Sienne," in "Ne dormons plus, il est temps de se lever," op. cit., pp. 105–25, at p. 106). On Catherine's mysticism, see also M. Zimmer, "'Two Bodies with One Soul': Catherine of Siena's Incarnational Model of Christian Mysticism," in Studia Mystica 19 (1998), pp. 21–35.

8. The intelligence of the Christian mystics "is first of all nourished by the revealed divine truth: it is faith, not emotion, that dominates their life" (R. Garrigou-Lagrange, L'unione mistica in S. Caterina da Siena, Firenze, 1938, p. 27).

9. Letters, III, p. 280 (Lettere, I, p. 9).

form of the language but with its content and her mode of expression—free of any artistic quest[10]—was essentially oratorial and not poetical.

Enamored with truth, Catherine tried to communicate it in the clearest possible way, even at the cost of being repetitive. While she made use of images in many cases, this was done only with the aim of explaining the truth as clearly as possible. Though these images at times seem poetical, the predominant character of her writings remains oratorial. Nonetheless, her oratorial writing is very often full of vigor and great beauty, revealing Catherine's considerable ability in constructing sentences, her rapid and concise style that seemed to derive from the same activity of her spirit, with its natural ability to grasp and clarify essential themes.

Despite Catherine's lack of precise philosophical notions, the doctrinal element continues to remain the true and real structure underpinning her dictations, which reveal her "powerful habit of reasoning," as vividly remarked by Giovanni Getto.[11] The doctrinal latticework, the presence of dogmatic content, and her powerful habit of meditation are also made manifest in the way in which Catherine makes use of images, which are drawn from both human realities and the world of nature and are found in her dictations in the form of various modes of expression that go from mere similarity to metaphor and allegory.

Her frequent resorting to metaphorical language to express the world of virtues and vices is not readily found in other mystics. Thus, Catherine does not limit herself to affirming that self-love is a "cloud" or that conscience is a "dog," but she makes use of these images by having the metaphorical term almost invariably at the beginning,

---

10. Her style is simple, "as rigorous as hardly elegant" (G. Berceville, "'L'amour sans gloses'—Actualité de Catherine de Sienne," in É. J. Lacelle (ed.), *Ne dormons plus, il est temps de se lever,*" op. cit., pp. 211–14, at p. 204), and even "harsh" (M. Ozilou and G. Berceville, "Théologie médiévale," in J.-Y. Lacoste (ed.), *Histoire de la théologie*, Paris, 2009, pp. 153–282, at p. 274).

11. G. Getto, *Letteratura religiosa del Trecento*, op. cit., p. 149.

which leads to such expressions as "the cloud of self-love" or "the dog of the conscience." All of Catherine's writings are marked by such manners of speaking (the so-called metaphors of specification):[12] "the cell of knowledge of oneself," "the eye of the intellect," "the pupil of the faith," "the ship of the soul," and many others. These metaphorical manners of speaking that consistently recur seem like formulas in which Catherine holds a conquered truth, and they reveal themselves as important points of support in her meditative process.

Catherine's language shows all the characteristics of religious meditation: it cannot be reduced to pure incitement, but it is an exhortative drive unleashed from a complex doctrinal foundation that reveals her reasoning habit. This doctrinal structure, the basis of all her expressions, has its own unmistakable originality and oratorial value. Catherine's language is therefore a privileged way of understanding her spirituality and the mystical inspiration that nourishes it.

4. CONCLUSION

According to the best literary criticism, Catherine's writings, though not poetically inspired, are characterized by a lively spirituality. Catherine's mysticism is a profound and personal understanding of revealed truths, which expresses itself in a language that shows how deeply rooted the saint's reflections are in a solid doctrinal framework, which comes from the Patristic and Scholastic tradition. Moreover, Catherine's images allow a glimpse of her meditative habit and the coherence of her mystical thought.

---

12. On the metaphors of specification in Catherine's writings, see R. Librandi, "Dal lessico delle Lettere di Caterina da Siena: la concretezza della fusione," in L. Leonardi and P. Trifone (eds.), *Dire l'ineffabile*, op. cit., pp. 19–40. (At p. 31, Librandi observes that these metaphors frequently occur in the *Letters*, and probably Catherine is at the origin of their use in the writings by other female mystics.)

The majority of scholars have also recognized that these writings reveal Catherine's striking and unmistakable personality, conferring on them a singular mark of unity. While their doctrinal content is that of tradition, their tone is quite original. This novelty of tone signals a unique personality capable of transforming and infusing new life into the heritage of tradition. This tone is fundamentally the same in all of Catherine's works and depends on a spiritual unity that expresses her inner life.

It is this unity of tone that postulates the individuality of their author. This unity of style manifests a spiritual unity grounded in a personal and unique mystical inspiration: ultimately, this mystical inspiration provides the undeniably unified character of all her writings. The unity of her mystical inspiration should certainly not be understood in the sense that the saint had only one mystical experience, but in the sense that her mysticism is uniform and always identical to itself, without change, and in this way is reflected in her writings.

Chapter 12

The Central Role of Discretion in Catherine's Spirituality

1. INTRODUCTION

This last and brief chapter examines the essential feature of Catherine's discretion, namely its being the core around which the saint's thinking is built and the necessary condition for safeguarding that unity in which Catherine joined together contemplation and an active life, exemplifying that ecclesial and apostolic dimension proper to the experience of Christian spirituality.

2. DISCRETION AS THE ESSENTIAL CONDITION OF UNITY IN CATHERINE'S SPIRITUALITY

To understand the structuring role of discretion as the element of unity in Catherine's spirituality, it is necessary to recapitulate in broad terms the primary elements of her thought. As was recalled earlier, Catherine's mysticism is not at all irrational but a profound and personal reflection on the revealed truths. This mysticism, though rich in language with overlapping images, is easily understandable. Despite the absence of systematic exposition, once the intricate tangle of images is unraveled, the saint's writings reveal clear and coherent thoughts.

Saint Catherine lived God's presence as a mystic, experiencing union with God. In her works, she very often refers to this union and the spiritual itinerary to attain it. Catherine was firmly convinced that man could reach this union, because the greatest gift from God to the creature endowed with reason is the capacity to know and love him. The crucial importance of knowing the truth to gain salvation derives from the fact that it is only in knowing the truth that one can come to love it as good.

Catherine was animated by the conviction that man needs to know himself and God. This is certainly not a rare theme in the history of theology, but in Catherine's spirituality it plays a central role that is unique. Her call to inhabit the "cell of the soul" in the "house of knowledge," to mention just a couple of images, constantly resurfaces in her writings and shows how this knowledge is absolutely necessary for the spiritual life. True knowledge is not purely natural knowledge because it can only result from the conjunction of reason and faith. Furthermore, it is more of a continual process than an isolated act: the soul must always inhabit the "cell of knowledge" because only by dwelling in this inner abode can one know the truth about man and God.

Dwelling in this constant inner life, man attains the knowledge of his nonbeing and recognizes his ontological dependence on God, who alone "is." These two axioms are the starting points of Catherine's intuition of being. Hers is a theocentric mystical vision: God is the supreme Being from whom everything that is has its life and, since it is created, participates in that Being. Hers is also an ethical vision: human wretchedness and human sins are contrasted with the greatness and goodness of God. In the *Dialogue*, one reads that the soul, in the dignity of her existence,

> tastes the immeasurable goodness and uncreated love with which I [i.e. God] created her. And in the sight of her own wretchedness she discovers and tastes my mercy.[1]

---

1. *Dialogue*, p. 104, ch. 51 (*Dialogo*, pp. 135–36).

The saint's mystical view is entirely centered on God as one and tri-une. The fact that the foundation of her spirituality is Christocentric does not take anything away from her theocentrism, since Catherine sees Christ as the bridge, the mediator between man and God, and the only path of salvation to attain union with the Trinity.

It is only on true knowledge, which man reaches by joining reason and faith, that the spiritual life can flourish. This twofold knowledge of man and God leads to the characteristic theme of unity because these two forms of knowledge may be distinguished in theory but are inseparable in practice. Indeed, knowledge of oneself without knowledge of God leads man to confusion and despair, while knowledge of God without knowledge of oneself and one's own sins leads to conceit.

This knowledge is true because it leads to knowing God—who is the "first sweet Truth"—and to man knowing himself in God: the truth of creation and ontological dependence on God and the truth of redemption by the blood Christ shed for the salvation of man. In letter 102, Catherine writes to Raymond of Capua that it is in knowing ourselves that "we know that we are not, but find our being in God, seeing that God created us in his image and likeness," and that

> in self-knowledge we discover also how God created us anew when he re-created us to grace in the blood of his only-begotten Son. That blood reveals to us the truth of God the Father. And his truth was this, that he created us for the glory and praise of his name, so that we might be made holy in him. What shows us that this is the truth? The blood of the spotless Lamb.[2]

Only true knowledge can provide proper direction to what Catherine calls the "affection of love," which is to say that natural tendency that drives the soul to love by spurring it to seek the object of its innate need for love, because the soul is "a tree made for love and

2. *Letters*, IV, p. 346 (*Lettere*, II, p. 127).

living only by love."[3] Thus, if love is grounded in knowledge, which directs and nourishes it, then as love increases faith—the "light of the intellect"—love ends up augmenting knowledge itself through a reciprocal circularity because "love follows upon understanding:" the more they know the more they love, and the more they love the more they know.[4]

The capacity to know and love God is made manifest in the three faculties of the soul: memory, intellect, and will. As was observed before,[5] Catherine thanks God for having created man in his image and likeness, giving the soul the ability to unite with the three divine Persons of the Trinity by way of its three faculties. The theme of unity is found in the understanding of the soul as reflecting the likeness of God in its unity and its three faculties. In the *Dialogue*, "the high and eternal Father" affirms:

> It pleased me to create you in my image and likeness with great providence. I provided you with the gift of memory so that you might hold fast my benefits and be made a sharer in my own, the eternal Father's power. I gave you understanding so that in the wisdom of my only-begotten Son you might comprehend and know what I the eternal Father want, I who gave you graces with such burning love. I gave you a will to love, making you a sharer in the Holy Spirit's mercy, so that you might love what your understanding sees and knows.[6]

One is in the grace of God only when unity and harmony exist among memory, intellect, and will, which is to say when the three faculties are "united among themselves that whatever the one wants the others follow."[7] This unity of the three faculties is so essential to this

---

3. *Dialogue*, p. 41, ch. 10 (*Dialogo*, p. 29).
4. *Dialogue*, p. 157, ch. 85 (*Dialogo*, p. 226).
5. See above all the references to *Prayers* 17 (X), 22 (XVII), 11 (XXI), and 4 (XXIII).
6. *Dialogue*, p. 277, ch. 135 (*Dialogo*, p. 430).
7. *Prayers*, 12, p. 116 (*Orazioni*, XXII, p. 256).

spiritual itinerary that, when describing the ascesis of the soul in the *Dialogue*, Catherine first of all considers the three major steps of Christ-the-bridge along this journey of ascent to be the reconciliation of the three faculties of the soul and their reunification in charity. It is only when the soul has recovered charity in the order and unity of its three faculties that one can attempt to rise and grow in charity. At that point, those major steps will still be considered the symbol of ascent, but no longer as faculties; rather, they are states of the soul in its ascent toward a perfect love for Christ-the-bridge. Catherine considers this journey of ascent to be, first, the reunification and harmonizing of the three faculties in charity, showing that, to reach this state (which she calls "common charity," or the level of charity that is absolutely necessary for man to be in a state of divine grace), the soul must exercise the virtues in the harmonious unity of the three faculties. Thus one reads in the *Dialogue*:

> When these three powers of the soul are gathered together, I [i.e. God] am in their midst by grace. And as soon as you are filled with my love and love of your neighbor, you will find yourself in the company of the multitude of solid virtues.[8]

It is through the three faculties that one can both know and love the truth, as the knowledge of God—the "first sweet Truth"—translates into the love of God. The true knowledge of the truth, which for Catherine is primarily a contemplative knowledge leading to know and love God, should by extension become a practical knowledge guiding virtuous action. In letter 102, Catherine writes to Raymond of Capua that she longed to see him "truly espoused to truth, a lover and follower of that truth."[9]

Discretion derives from true knowledge. On the one hand, it leads man to see and know as discernment, teaching him how to

---

8. *Dialogue*, p. 108, ch. 54 (*Dialogo*, p. 142).
9. *Letters*, IV, p. 346 (*Lettere*, II, p. 127).

distinguish and judge values; on the other hand, it is not simply limited to this aspect of knowledge, as it also drives man to act in conformity with this discernment, by rendering his debt to all. Therefore, discretion turns man not only into a lover but also into a follower of the truth.

Within Catherine's spirituality, discretion is a bond of unity between mysticism and morality because it unites her mystical understanding of God as the true and good Being from whom all of creation derives with the ethical understanding of the wretchedness of human sins and the consequent necessity of virtuous moral action for salvation. Even beyond this union of mysticism and morality, discretion is always structured as a bond of unity because it unites discernment—which is derived as practical knowledge from the true knowledge that results from the conjunction of reason and faith—with moral action, as a fundamental feature of all virtuous action and therefore as a condition for the unity of the virtues. In fact, discretion not only enlightens the soul as a "discreet light" by showing it how to render the debt to God, to itself, and to its neighbor but also drives it to do so in the most appropriate manner and measure, as the seasoning of every virtue in its guiding role in the moral and spiritual life.

For Catherine, discretion has its source in charity, which remains the source of every virtue. Nonetheless, its importance is so great that it participates—together with charity—in the genesis of every virtue. In describing the soul as a "tree of love" in the *Dialogue*, Catherine sets the little shoot of discretion alongside the trunk of this tree, such that all the fruits of the tree are seasoned with discretion because they are united together. This image of discretion as a condition for the unity of the virtues is also found in letter 213, where one reads that all the fruits of the virtues arise from the "branches of discretion" that come out of the tree of charity.

In conclusion, in Catherine's spiritual reflection, discretion is the essential condition of unity between mysticism and morality, applying discernment (which derives from the true knowledge that is the fruit of the saint's mystical experience) to the whole moral and spiritual life. It thereby shows how thoroughly intertwined mysticism and morality are in her spirituality and how discretion is the seal on this harmonious encounter. Furthermore, beyond the mystical and moral perspective, discretion reveals itself as a condition of unity of the virtues by uniting discernment with moral action.

It is precisely in this function of structuring unity that discretion reveals itself as the core of the entire spirituality of Saint Catherine.

3. DISCRETION AT THE CORE OF CATHERINE'S SPIRITUALITY

From the ethical and spiritual character of her writings, it clearly emerges that Catherine's purpose is essentially parenetic, as her teaching is primarily aimed at showing the moral conduct to be pursued to attain union with God. Her teaching shows the importance of the moral life to achieve spiritual perfection and is grounded in a moral structure regulated by discretion, which itself reveals the moral dimension of Catherine's spirituality.

Catherine uses various images to represent discretion, such as that of the shoot, the little sapling planted in the ground of true humility, and grafted into the tree of charity, which participates in the genesis of the virtues that come out of the tree seasoned by discretion. In this image, discretion is presented as a prerequisite for the virtues, even before being the condition for their unity, by guiding them and conferring right measure on them in the fulfillment of virtuous acts.

The images of light and knowledge express the function of discretion in discerning the truth. This discerning aspect of discretion is so important that Catherine identifies the "root of discretion" with true knowledge.[10] Nevertheless, as was repeatedly stressed throughout this study, discretion is not limited to discernment alone but is also the proper effect of this discernment in that it leads to its concrete

10. *Dialogue*, p. 40, ch. 9 (*Dialogo*, p. 28).

fulfillment in the virtuous action. Catherine's discretion may there-fore be defined as knowledge and love of the truth *in action*, namely that knowledge and love of the truth (which is God) that leads con-cretely to the virtuous action. It is the practice of discretion that leads man to dwell in the divine grace, to unify his three faculties (memory, intellect, and will), and to advance in charity.

Catherine's insistence on dwelling in the cell of knowledge, on being not only lovers but also followers of the truth, reveals the importance that she attributes to discretion. Dwelling in the knowl-edge of the truth makes us free, as knowing the truth leads us to loving it, and loving it frees us from the slavery of mortal sin. This presupposes the intervention of discretion: while the knowledge of oneself and God is attained when the light of reason is accompanied by the light of faith that allows man to "see," remaining in this "spiri-tual sight" is accomplished through the exercise of the virtues and therefore through the intervention of discretion.

For Catherine, therefore, it is necessary to dwell in knowledge to be lovers and followers of the truth in the exercise of the virtues, according to the manner and measure indicated by discretion. In this role, discretion fulfills its primary function, which is that of render-ing the debt to God, oneself, and one's neighbor. In rendering the debt to God, discretion regulates charity insofar as, according to Catherine, one must love God without setting law or limit, while one's neighbor must be loved with "ordered charity," which is to say by sacrificing material goods for the life of others and even of oneself, without however sacrificing one's own spiritual good, because this would entail an offense against God. The "discreet" soul must also render the debt to itself through the hatred of vice and of its own sensuality: in this, discretion is a "knife" that "kills and cuts off all selfish love to its foundation in self-will."[11] This love of self is that perverse and disordered love that, through the involvement of both

---

11. *Dialogue*, p. 43, ch. 11 (*Dialogo*, p. 33).

the intellect and the will, leads to loving oneself for the sake of one-self rather than loving oneself for the sake of God. This self-love

> takes away the light of reason and keeps us from knowing the truth. It robs us of the life of grace and gives us death. It deprives us of liberty and makes us servants and slaves of sin.[12]

Catherine's frequent reminders to open the "eye of the intel-lect" to gain a "spiritual sight" imply a will to see, which can only be attained after removing the "cloud of self-love" through the exercise of the virtues. To do this, one needs the "knife of discretion," which is a double-edged knife of hatred and love: hatred of sin and love of virtue. Leading man to exercise the virtues, discretion thus frees him from the slavery of mortal sin and makes it possible for man's will to be united with the will of God.

4. CONCLUSION

In summary, three are the fundamental aspects of Catherine's discre-tion: its central place in her writings, its originality,[13] and the role it plays in interpreting the unity of her teaching.

Unlike the spiritual writers who preceded her, in whose reflec-tions discretion/prudence is one theme among many, for Catherine discretion is truly the structuring notion of her whole thinking, the core around which her entire spirituality is organized. The original manner in which the saint makes use of this notion lies precisely in this structuring role.

---

12. Letter 299: *Letters*, III, pp. 160–61 (*Lettere*, IV, p. 255).
13. One can perfectly apply to the whole of Catherine's teaching this profound truth expressed by C. S. Lewis: "No man who values originality will ever be original. But try to tell the truth as you see it, try to do any bit of work as well as it can be done for the work's sake, and what men call originality will come unsought" ("Membership," in W. Hooper (ed.), *Fern-Seed and Elephants and Other Essays on Christianity by C. S. Lewis*, Glasgow, 1975, pp. 11–25, at p. 25).

Catherine's hallmark is unity, from the undeniably unified character of her writings (which, in turn, reveal a spiritual unity that is the expression of a unique mystical inspiration) to union with God, which she experienced in life and to which she desired to show other souls the spiritual path, as the aim toward which all her teachings converge. Along this spiritual journey, discretion comes to be an essential condition for the unity between discernment (which derives from the knowledge and love of truth) and the virtuous action that is indispensable to attain union with God. In this sense, Catherine's discretion is knowledge and love of the truth *in action*. Combining discernment with its concrete fulfillment in virtuous action, discretion ends up being the condition for man's true freedom. By making him abide in the love of truth, discretion frees man from the slavery of sin and allows him to remain in the divine grace and grow in charity. It is therefore through discretion that man acquires his true freedom.

While the knowledge and love of the truth is the primary characteristic of Catherine's thinking, the core of her reflection is centered on discretion, which leads man to act in accordance with this knowledge and love of the truth, thereby uniting this knowledge and love with virtuous and free action. In this, Catherine is truly the teacher of discretion, both in her writings and in the example set by her life.

General Conclusions

fatti non foste a viver come bruti,
ma per seguir virtute e conoscenza.

(Dante, *Divine Comedy*, Hell, XXVI:120)[1]

The richness of Catherine's life and writings has been a powerful source of inspiration throughout the centuries. This wealth shines forth from a study of the notion of discretion, as the summary conclusions of this research amply confirm.

1. SUMMARY CONCLUSIONS

(i) Textual Criticism

As a logical premise to the investigation of the significance of discretion in Catherine's writings, the first part of this study addressed the question of their authenticity.

Scholars agree that Catherine was illiterate (though not uncultured),[2] perhaps able at most to read with difficulty. The credibility

---

1. "You were not made to live like brutes, but to pursue virtue and knowledge." These words, spoken by the soul of Ulysses in Dante's masterpiece, capture the indissoluble unity of knowledge and virtuous action so typical of Catherine.

2. This important distinction was highlighted in the process that led to the elevation of Catherine to Doctor of the Church: her writings are the work of an illiterate (in that she did not attend any school) but learned person (as attested by her terminological and conceptual precision). See "Votum alterius censoris theologici," in *Urbis et orbis*, op. cit., pp. 29–45, at pp. 31–32.

of her miraculous writing, recounted in the final part of letter 272 to Raymond of Capua in the autumn 1377 while she was at Tentennano castle, is controversial. What can be stated with certainty is that no autographical writing by the saint has ever been found and that she dictated to amanuenses of different levels of learning and training, who later transcribed her dictations and collected them in various manuscripts. Hence, whenever referring to Catherine's "original" writings, one does not mean to refer to autographical writings, but to authentic writings that several disciples wrote down from her dictations.

As Catherine's dictations have been collected in disciples' manuscripts, some scholars have assumed that minor alterations may have occurred either at the moment of dictation or later, when transcribed into manuscripts. Yet, this is no more than a theory. The only evidence is that the disciples removed from several letters information of a purely personal and private character.

In summary, while admitting the possibility of minor alterations, scholars recognize the substantial authenticity of Catherine's writings, essentially for two reasons: the disciples' respect for Catherine's dictations (which they considered to be of supernatural origin) and the undeniably unified character impressed upon all of the writings by her unmistakable style.

(ii) Textual Analysis

Catherine's writings were then examined in the second part of this study to reach a definition of *discretion* that would faithfully reflect her teaching. This second part was replete with quotations so as to let Catherine speak for herself. The finding was that, despite the occasional imprecisions and repetitions, and once her tangled images have been unraveled, Catherine's reflections breathe life into a uniform and coherent body of teaching.

In her writings, Catherine articulates the moral conduct to be pursued to attain union with God. Her teaching is built upon a moral structure regulated by discretion, the pin on which her entire spirituality hinges. Within this context, the knowledge of truth—the truth about man and God—is the natural starting point of discretion. For Catherine, when the truth is known by the intellect enlightened by the light of faith, it attracts the soul as the object of its innate need for love. This is so because man, created in the image and likeness of God, was endowed with the capacity to know and love God through his three faculties (memory, intellect, and will).

In Catherine's reflection, there is a close connection between being and knowing. For her, man depends on God not just in his being but also in his knowledge of the truth, since being and truth are one and the same in God. Just as man can exist only by way of participation, so man can know the truth only by way of participation, receiving the light of faith, because the truth—which is God—exists independently of man's existence and knowledge. In other words, Catherine explicitly acknowledges not only man's ontological dependence on God but also his dependence on God for knowing the truth.

Knowledge leads to loving the truth in a reciprocal and continuous cycle, since for Catherine love follows the intellect: the more it knows the more it loves, and the more it loves the more it knows. This knowledge is speculative but becomes practical insofar as it guides and regulates moral and spiritual action. Practical knowledge coincides with the discerning aspect of discretion. Discretion, however, is not limited to discernment alone but includes also the effect of discernment, leading it to its concrete fulfillment in virtuous action. In this way, discretion in Catherine becomes knowledge and love of the truth *in action* and, as such, the core of the whole moral and spiritual life.

The analysis of Catherine's writings has thus made it possible to point out the central role of discretion in this saint's spirituality and, at the same time, its complexity, which makes it rather reductive to refer to it with the term *discernment*. In fact, the analysis of many passages in the *Dialogue*, the *Letters*, and the *Prayers* shows that discretion is much more than mere discernment: rather, it is the concrete fulfillment of discernment in virtuous action. In this, rendering the debt is the primary act of discretion because, according to Catherine, once discernment (derived from true knowledge) has shown man what he must give, as well as the way of giving and to whom, all the operations of the soul should be carried out with the one and only purpose of rendering the debt.

Finally, the analysis of the text has confirmed that the two terms *discretion* and *prudence* have the same meaning in Catherine.

(iii) Sources of Catherine's Discretion

In its being not only discernment but also the fulfillment of what should be done in practice in accordance with the manner and measure established by discernment, Catherine's discretion is the heir of a long Christian tradition.

While the tradition of *discretio spirituum* is reflected in some passages of Catherine's writings, particularly those on the discernment of visions, it is primarily the tradition of *discretio* and prudence that is a plausible source of Catherine's reflection on discretion. Though it is almost impossible to identify exactly which authors mostly influenced her, Catherine is likely to have had indirect knowledge of a number of spiritual writings by listening to preaching and through her contacts with religious men of various orders, particularly Dominicans. The impact on her of the earlier tradition is obvious, but Catherine is unique for the central role that discretion occupies in her spirituality.

(iv) Catherine's Discretion between Mysticism and Morality

Finally, in the fourth part of this study, Catherine's teaching was depicted as a cognitive result of the mystical inspiration that nourished her spiritual reflection. Having experienced God's presence as a mystic, Catherine refers quite often in her writings to the union with God while pointing to the moral conduct to be followed to attain it. Her teachings are supported by a moral structure regulated by discretion.

In Catherine, discretion is not only at the core of her spiritual reflection but also the bond of unity between mysticism and morality. It is discretion that unites the mystical understanding of God as the true and good Being with man's ethical understanding of the wretchedness of sin and the need for moral action in view of salvation.

2. FURTHER FINDINGS: DISCRETION AS A PRIVILEGED TOOL FOR INTERPRETING CATHERINE'S SPIRITUALITY

In addition to these results arrived at in the four parts of this study, others were perhaps initially unexpected but have come out as equally important findings.

(i) Catherine as Mystic of the Truth

An in-depth analysis of the notion of discretion allows the full appreciation of how the truth is really "the characteristic of the life, thought and style of St. Catherine."[3] In the course of this study, it was repeatedly emphasized how true knowledge, which is knowledge of the truth, is the starting point in Catherine's reflection: truth about man (his ontological dependence and the wretchedness of sin) and truth about God (his supreme being and his infinite love, through which he created man in his image and likeness, offering him the possibility of redemption and salvation through the incarnation of the Word).

God's being and his truth certainly do not depend on man and man's knowledge. To the contrary, it is man that depends on God not only for his being but also for his knowledge of the truth, which, once it is known, is loved and guides man toward what is good. Knowledge of the truth, which leads to love of the truth, becomes by extension

---

3. See G. Cavallini's introduction to the *Dialogo*, p. xxxi.

that discernment that leads to its concrete application as practical knowledge in the virtuous action. In this way, discretion—as knowledge and love of the truth *in action*—emerges in the fullness of its role in guiding moral and spiritual action along that path that alone can lead to salvation: the path of Christ-the-bridge leading to union with God.[4]

Catherine, the lover of the truth, embracing discretion as the core of her spiritual reflection shows that there is an absolute truth to be applied to moral and spiritual action as soon as it has become known and loved. It is precisely this passion for the truth that turns Catherine of Siena into an "embarrassing" saint: she causes uneasiness because, as an attentive scholar has efficaciously remarked,

> truth is a word that frightens.... The very concept of truth is criticized, it is systematically avoided in the discourse of many of our contemporaries.[5]

(ii) Catherine as Doctor of Unity

When investigating the significance and scope of Catherine's discretion, one discovers another aspect that characterizes her spirituality, on account of which Catherine can rightly be called "doctor of unity."

This characteristic feature is already manifested in her unity of style, which reveals a spiritual unity that depends on her own mystical inspiration. It is precisely this mystical inspiration that gives Catherine's writings their undeniably unified character. Having lived God's presence as a mystic, experiencing union with God, Catherine teaches unity both through the example of her life and through her

---

4. In Catherine's writings, the highest number (forty-three) of citations to the New Testament is to John 14:6, where Christ reveals himself as the way, the truth, and the life.

5. G. Berceville, "'L'amour sans gloses,'" op. cit., p. 202.

writings, where she indicates the moral conduct to be pursued to attain union with God. In her moral teaching, discretion plays a central role, as the condition of unity between discernment and its concrete fulfillment in the virtuous action and in the unifying connection of the virtues.

Catherine's quest for unity—starting with the structural unity of the soul and its three faculties (memory, intellect, and will) that reflect the likeness of the one and triune God—never detracts from necessary distinctions. Thus, the same act of discretion in the virtuous action— the rendering of the debt—is distinguished by Catherine into rendering the debt to God, to oneself, and to one's neighbor, the primacy of the first debt being confirmed by the fact that the two others follow from it as their consequence.

In Catherine, sin is dissected into the three enemies of the soul (self, world, and devil), which, if not resisted, lead man into the darkness of sin, depriving him of that light of faith that, when added to the light of natural reason, allows him to see. It is only with discretion, exercising the virtues in the harmonious unity of the three faculties, that man can maintain his spiritual sight and abide in the twofold knowledge of self and of God. This last distinction, too, is at the service of a unified truth: knowledge is twofold (and therefore the result of distinction), but there is only one true knowledge, because the knowledge of self and of the wretchedness of sin leads to despair if it is not accompanied by the knowledge of God, and, conversely, the knowledge of God leads to conceit if it is not accompanied by the knowledge of self.

(iii) Catherine as Champion of Freedom

By leading man to exercise the virtues, discretion frees him from the slavery of mortal sin and makes it possible to unite his will with God's.[6] It is therefore discretion that permits man to acquire his true

---

6. As Cardinal Biffi has aptly noted, all too often forms of true slavery are falsely advertised as new modes of freedom. See G. Biffi, *Una sorte bellissima. Piccolo Dizionario del Cristianesimo* (E. Ghini, ed.), Casale Monferrato, 2003 (new edn. 2004), p. 126.

freedom.[7] The Second Vatican Council reaffirmed that true freedom is "an outstanding manifestation of the divine image in humans."[8]

Thus combining both knowledge and love of the truth in the virtuous action, discretion turns out to be the prerequisite for man's freedom, confirming the importance of the relationship between truth and freedom, a fundamental and universal theme as reaffirmed by the Synod of Bishops in 1991:

> the question of the relation of freedom to truth, which modern European culture has often conceived in opposition to each other, seems very important, since in fact freedom and truth are ordered to each other in such a way that neither can be achieved without the other.[9]

In this teaching, too, which is valid in all places and at all times, Christian doctrine finds a solid foundation in Catherine's thought, which still speaks to the man of today with the same intensity with which it was originally uttered in the fourteenth century.

7. In the footsteps of the rigorous lesson by the Servant of God Father Tomas Tyn, OP (1950–1990), G. Cavalcoli has warned how urgent it is to free liberty from its false conceptions (*La liberazione della libertà. Il messaggio di P. Tomas Tyn ai giovani*, Verona, 2008, p. 7).

8. Second Vatican Council, "Pastoral Constitution on the Church in the World of Today" (*Gaudium et spes*), December 7, 1965, in N. P. Tanner (ed.), *Decrees of the Ecumenical Councils. Volume Two: Trent to Vatican II*, London and Washington, DC, 1990, pp. 1069–135, at p. 1078, para. 17. It is precisely the lack of this connection between truth and freedom that is at the origin of today's spiritual crisis. See C. Caffarra, *L'amore insidiato. "Non è bene che l'uomo sia solo." L'amore, il matrimonio, la famiglia nella prospettiva cristiana*, vol. 2 (R. Ansani, ed.), Siena, 2008, p. 58.

9. Final Declaration "*Ut testes simus Christi qui nos liberavit*," Special Assembly for Europe of the Synod of Bishops (November 28–December 14, 1991), in *L'Osservatore Romano* (English edn., December 23/30, 1991), pp. 3–4 and 13–14, at p. 4.

SELECT BIBLIOGRAPHY

Over the last decades, new standard editions of the *Dialogue* and the *Prayers* have been published in Italian, and new translations of all Catherine's writings have appeared in English and French:

(i) Italian

Cavallini, G. (ed.) S. Caterina da Siena, *Il Dialogo* (2nd edn.), Siena, 1995. (The first edition was published in Rome in 1968.)

Cavallini, G. (ed.) S. Caterina da Siena, *Le Orazioni*, Roma, 1978. (Of this work, there is also an edition published in Siena in 1993, which is essentially the same as the 1978 edition but without the Latin text.)

A critical edition of the *Letters* has been in the making for quite some time but is not yet available in print. Hence the standard edition (despite its flaws) remains:

Misciatelli, P. (ed.) *Le lettere di S. Caterina da Siena ridotte a miglior lezione e in ordine nuovo disposte con note di N. Tommaseo*, 6 vols., Siena 1913–1922 (reprinted in Florence, 1939–1940).

An indispensable working tool is today the CD-ROM produced under the auspices of the Roman Province of the Dominican order, incorporating Giuliana Cavallini's critical edition of the *Dialogue* and the *Prayers* and Antonio Volpato's text of the *Letters*:

Sbaffoni, F. (ed.) Santa Caterina da Siena, *Opera Omnia. Testi e Concordanze*, Pistoia, 2002.

(ii) English

Noffke, S. (ed.) Catherine of Siena, *The Dialogue*, New York, Ramsey, and Toronto, 1980.
Noffke, S. (ed.) *The Letters of Catherine of Siena*, Tempe, AZ, 4 vols.: 2000, 2001, 2007, and 2008. (The first volume is an updated version of the 1988 edition.)
Noffke, S. (ed.) *The Prayers of Catherine of Siena* (2nd edn.), Lincoln, NE, 2001.

(iii) French

Portier, L. (ed.) Catherine de Sienne, *Le Dialogue* (2nd edn.), Paris, 1999 (1st edn.: Paris 1992).
Portier, L. (ed.) Catherine de Sienne, *Les Oraisons*, Paris, 1992.

A new French translation of the *Letters* is under way, of which *Les Éditions du Cerf* have published five volumes at the time of writing:

Catherine de Sienne *Les Lettres* (M. Raiola, tr.), Paris, 2008 (vol. 1: "Lettres aux papes Grégoire XI et Urbain VI aux cardinaux et aux évêques"), 2010 (vol. 2: "Lettres aux rois, aux reines et aux responsables politiques" and vol. 3: "Lettres aux laïcs (1)"), and 2012 (vol. 4: "Lettres aux laïcs (2)" and vol. 5: "À la famille, aux disciples et aux 'mantellate'").

Comprehensive bibliographical references are in the five volumes published under the auspices of what is now the International Center for the Study of Saint Catherine (*Centro Internazionale di Studi Cateriniani*), which cover the publications of the twentieth century:

Zanini, L. *Bibliografia analitica di S. Caterina da Siena, 1901–1950*, Roma, 1971.
Zanini, L. *Bibliografia analitica di S. Caterina da Siena, 1951–1975*, Roma, 1985.
Paterna, M. C. *Bibliografia analitica di S. Caterina da Siena, 1976–1985*, Roma, 1989.

Paterna, M. C. *Bibliografia analitica di S. Caterina da Siena, 1986–1990*, Roma, 2000.

Paterna, M. C. *Bibliografia analitica di S. Caterina da Siena, 1991–2000*, Roma, 2003.

Among the introductory works, in English, on Catherine's life and spirituality, see:

Cavallini, G. *Catherine of Siena*, London and New York, 1998 and 2005.

D'Urso, G. *Catherine of Siena. Doctor of the Church (Notes on Her Life and Teaching)* (T. McDermott, tr.), Chicago, 2013.

Fatula, M. A. *Catherine of Siena's Way* (revised edn.), Collegeville, MN, 1990.

Sr. M. Jeremiah*The Secret of the Heart. A Theological Study of Catherine of Siena's Teaching on the Heart of Jesus*, Front Royal, VA, 1995.

McDermott, T. *Catherine of Siena. Spiritual Development in Her Life and Teaching*, New York and Mahwah, NJ, 2008.

Noffke, S. *Catherine of Siena—Vision through a Distant Eye*, Collegeville, MN, 1996. (This book was reprinted in Lincoln, NE, in 2006.)

O'Driscoll, M. T. *Catherine of Siena—Passion for the Truth, Compassion for Humanity*, New Rochelle, NY, 1993.

Three volumes with which any student of Catherine may want to be familiar are:

Kearns, C. (ed.) Raymond of Capua, *The Life of Catherine of Siena*, Wilmington, DE, 1980.

Laurent, M.-H. (ed.) "Il Processo Castellano, con appendice di Documenti sul Culto e la Canonizzazione di S. Caterina da Siena," in R. Orestano et al. (eds.), *Fontes vitae S. Catherinæ senensis historici quos edidit Commissio editionibus Cathedrae Catharinae praefacta*, vol. 9, Milano, 1942.

Urbis et orbis concessionis tituli Doctoris, et extensionis eiusdem tituli ad universam Ecclesiam, necnon Officii et Missae de communi doctorum virginum, in honorem S. Catherinae Senensis, virginis, Tertii Ordinis S. Dominici (Sacra Rituum Congregatione, Michaele Browne, relatore), Città del Vaticano, 1969.

Among the writings consulted for this study on discretion/prudence, see:

Berceville, G. "La proclamation de Sainte Catherine Docteur de l'Église: une approche de théologie historique," in D. Giunta (ed.) , *Il servizio dottrinale di Caterina da Siena*, Firenze, 2012, 15–51.

Cavalcoli, G. M. "La vittoria sull''amor proprio' nella dottrina di S. Caterina da Siena," in *Divinitas* 44 (2001), pp. 3–16 (Part 1) and pp. 115–40 (Part 2).

Centi, T. S. "Luci e ombre sul tomismo di S. Caterina da Siena," in *Atti del Congresso Internazionale di Studi Cateriniani, Siena-Roma 24–29 aprile 1980*, Roma, 1981, pp. 76–92.

Dingjan, F. *Discretio. Les origines patristiques et monastiques de la doctrine sur la prudence chez saint Thomas d'Aquin*, Assen, 1967.

D'Urso, G. *Il genio di santa Caterina*, Roma, 1971.

Garrigou-Lagrange, R. *L'unione mistica in santa Caterina da Siena*, Firenze, 1938.

Getto, G. *Letteratura Religiosa del Trecento*, Firenze, 1967.

Mangano Ragazzi, G. *In obbedienza alla verità. La discrezione/prudenza come perno della spiritualità di Santa Caterina da Siena*, Siena, 2010.

Riccardi, C. *Il pensiero filosofico e mistico di S. Caterina da Siena*, Siena, 1994.

INDEX

In this index, there are no entries on such terms (except with accompanying qualifiers) as God, soul, truth, spirituality, discretion, prudence, light, and virtue, as they are the very focus of this monograph. Information that can easily be retrieved through the table of contents is not repeated here. To facilitate consultation, subentries have been avoided.